PREACHING AT THE PA
ASB GOSPELS—SUN
VOLUM

PREACHING AT THE PARISH COMMUNION

ASB Gospels—Sundays: Year Two, Volume Two

PETER MORRIS

MOWBRAY
LONDON & OXFORD

ISBN 0-264-67121-X

First published 1987
by A.R.Mowbray & Co. Ltd
Saint Thomas House, Becket Street
Oxford OX1 1SJ

British Library Cataloguing in Publication Data

Morris, Peter
Preaching at the parish communion : ASB
Gospels - Sundays : year two, volume two.
— (Mowbray's sermon outline series).
1. Church of England—Sermons 2. Church
year sermons—Outlines, syllabi, etc.
I. Title
251'.02 BX5133

ISBN 0-264-67121-X

Printed and bound in Great Britain by
Biddles Limited, Guildford, Surrey.

CONTENTS

FOREWORD

Some years ago, when I was Honorary Director of the College of Preachers, I was advised to make myself acquainted with the work of one called Peter Morris, at that time Incumbent of Sawbridgeworth in the Diocese of St Albans, and reputed to be gifted at producing the kind of attractive short address, with substance in it, that befits the Parish Communion setting. I took this advice and was not disappointed; indeed, I saw to it that this skill was made available to others from time to time on the staff of the College of Preachers.

Then I lost track of him; but our ways crossed a few years later when I was asked to conduct a Retreat at Pleshey in the Diocese of Chelmsford, for by then he had become Warden of this famous Retreat House, doing a fine job and being made an Honorary Canon of the Diocese. He is now in charge of a group of parishes at Ilketshall, Bungay, in Suffolk.

Maybe it is not surprising that when I was looking for a new writer in this series of preaching books, I should have thought of Peter Morris. I wondered if he had retained his skill at communicating with an ordinary parish congregation; and could it be that, as a result of his work at Pleshey, there would be added a new depth of spirituality and sensitivity to human need in his work? On inviting him to let me see some of his sermons I found this to be the case, and the result is this book. Some care has had to be taken to transpose his attractive speaking style into a written form without losing the life, but he has shown himself a quick learner. I am confident that those upon whom is laid the weekly burden and privilege of preaching will find inspiration and help in what he has written. It is thoughtful, down to earth and meets people where they are today.

D. W. CLEVERLEY FORD

NINTH SUNDAY BEFORE CHRISTMAS

Awareness and freedom

John 3.3 (*NEB*) '. . . *unless a man has been born over again he cannot see the Kingdom of God.*'

One hundred million pounds is a lot of money. Yet that amount was the total contributed in only one year by the people of Great Britain to relieve starvation in the famine-stricken lands of Africa. The year was 1985. Do you remember 'Band Aid' and 'Live Aid', and all that followed in those twelve months of giving on a lavish nationwide scale? It was as if a great floodgate of generosity had suddenly been opened, a phenomenon made all the more remarkable because the Englishman is not generally renowned for giving money to charity. His home is his castle and that is where his charity not only begins but so often (as many a door-to-door flag seller can testify), comes to a parsimonious end.

1 *Stabbed awake*

So what brought about such a radical change of attitude? What stabbed the Englishman awake? To change the metaphor back to the opening of a floodgate, what 'turned him on'? It is now common knowledge and part of any retrospective record of the year in question that, for the short space of a poignant television newsreel direct from Ethiopia, two worlds, miles apart, became one world. During those heart-rending moments as we watched close-ups of the dying children of a despairing people, we were inhabiting the same world and seeing it with a new awareness.

2 *Seeing with different eyes*

Analyse that renewed sense of awareness and what do you find? A great deal of guilt, a great deal of sympathy (and empathy), and an alertness to demands and responsibilities that hitherto lay dormant. With this awakening came a compelling need to translate it into action there and then. In all but a few cases this sense of urgency could only be assuaged by giving, and so the money came rolling in out of all kinds of motives, good, bad, but never indifferent.

Never indifferent. Not when once you have seen a situation with a new awareness. You are still living in the same old world but you are seeing it with different eyes.

I remember as a small child having been totally absorbed in some activity when I became suddenly conscious of, and nettled by the fact that, my mother was watching me. 'Don't look', I said; to which she had a stock reply, 'A cat may look at a king, I suppose'? Such was her invariable response, and I have often wondered, since discovering it for myself, whether she knew the other half of the adage – 'A cat may look at a king . . . *but it's not a king that the cat sees*'.

Awareness, then, for the cat *and* for the king. Without awareness you cannot experience the radical change of heart that brings in one hundred million pounds.

3 *Oh to go back across the years*

We have to face those things that stand in the way of our awareness, not only of the needs of the Third World, but of the world we inhabit personally each day, in the home, in the community, in the congregation. We are bound and partially blinded by our lifelong habits of thought and behaviour, by our traditions and prejudices, by our terrible fears and anxieties. We are bound, too, by our past with all its mistakes, its inadequacies and its guilt. As one gets older one can increasingly fall victim to that kind of regret.

Here are some of the words written by James Hastings during the First World War:

Oh to go back across the years long vanished
To have the words unsaid, the deeds undone,
The errors cancelled, the dark shadows banished,

In the glad sense of a new world begun;
To be a little child whose page of story
Is yet undimmed, unblotted by a stain,
And in the sunrise of primeval glory
To know that life has had its start again.[1]

The poet is imagining the feelings of an old man looking back on his life and torturing himself with a sense of unworthiness and irredeemable failure.

Oh to go back across the years and to know that life has had its start again!

4 *Born anew*

Were these the feelings of an old man who came to Jesus secretly under the cover of darkness? Nicodemus came, out of who knows what motives? But then our Lord does not ask of any seeker awkward questions about motives.

So, Nicodemus comes; half critical, half receptive and Jesus stabs him awake. 'You can only experience the Kingdom of God by becoming a child again. You, an old man, have to be born anew.'

A cynical theological student of my acquaintance used to say he could never 'get on' with St John's gospel because Jesus always seemed to him to be talking in riddles. This statement about being 'born anew' is surely an example of what that student meant – hard to comprehend and so easily misunderstood and misused. But Jesus' riddles are intended to help us find our answer, and on the way to find out what is binding, blinding, and stifling our freedom to be our true selves.

Nicodemus, a Pharisee, was hampered by the traditions of legalistic Judaism; he and Jesus belonged to two different worlds. The Pharisee looked upon a sinner as an unrepentant breaker of the law, but to Jesus he was one who was lost and must be found. So Nicodemus must be born anew. But

1. From *Greater Men and Women of the Bible*, volume 5, p.380.

perhaps he misunderstood (accidentally or deliberately), what was meant. Jesus explained and, in effect, told Nicodemus, as he tells us, that although physically we were children before we could become adults, we were not, so to speak, born fully human. We can only rise to become the full human beings God intends us to be when our vision is cleansed and we can see the world new and fresh like a child. Awareness is what we need. Awareness of life lying open at every point to God's Spirit. The first step towards that awakening is to make a conscious response to the one who is longing for our awakening. We need not go to him warily and by night, like Nicodemus, for God's time is always now and his charity endless.

EIGHTH SUNDAY BEFORE CHRISTMAS

In the wilderness

> John 3.14–15 (*RSV*) '*As Moses lifted up the serpent in the wilderness, so must the Son of Man be lifted up, that whoever believes in him may have eternal life.*'

For most of us who live in Britain now, the thought of displaced persons belongs to past history, part of the old wartime black and white newsreels distanced from us by almost half a century, except perhaps for some of us belonging to a particular generation, now in our late fifties, who were evacuees. The newsreels show troops of children setting off from city railway stations with their labels and gas-mask boxes slung round their necks on their way to an unknown, unfamiliar destination. For these people those distant events have a particular and personal significance. They, at least, will have some clue to what it means to be displaced persons, parted from their familiar home, apprehensive, bewildered, as are so many in today's conflict-ridden world.

1 *The wilderness*

Bewildered; in the wilderness; just as the Israelites were with Moses – displaced persons trekking through the desert on their way to a new home in an unfamiliar land. On that journey they encountered many hardships and afflictions. They suffered hunger and thirst and they were attacked by poisonous snakes. The dramatic story of it all in the Book of Numbers tells us in chapter 21 that Moses made a brass model of one of those fiery serpents and held it up on a pole, like a standard, for all to see. Anyone who was a victim of snake bite simply had to lift his head out there in the wilderness and he was cured. The very symbol of destruction became the means of healing.

This is the backdrop to the words of Jesus in today's gospel, and I want to give three words from that text particular emphasis; 'As Moses lifted up the serpent *in the wilderness*, so must the Son of Man be lifted up, that whoever believes in him may have eternal life.' The wilderness was the arena in which healing and life were given to all who were prepared to lift up their heads and look.

2 *'Come ye apart'*

It is deeply significant that when Jesus wanted his disciples to slow down from the constant demands of their ministry, and in so doing to confront new and lifegiving truths about themselves and God, he invited them to become displaced persons. 'Come ye apart' he said to them, 'into a desert place and rest.' And I expect they were as bewildered and apprehensive as those wartime evacuees. But although a desert place is a place of struggle and serpents, it is also a place of rest and stillness. The one is not contradictory to the other.

When you ask one of those wartime evacuees to look back and reflect upon the refugee experience of being moved away from their home into alien surroundings, more often than not they will speak of the good and valuable side of it all, rather than the pain and homesickness which were so evident at the time. For them, too, the wilderness experience in so many cases had its creative side.

For modern-day christians living in a frenetic, jet-propelled society, there is a desperate need, as there was for those first disciples, to lift our heads from the familiar routine and – for however short a space – to find our own wilderness. There is a need to find the place where we can slow down and yet become more aware; the place of stillness yet also the place where we can confront our own particular serpents of old resentments, recent hurts or nagging guilt; the place where we can recognise them, face them and be healed.

Our Lord's own ministry began there in the desert place where the darkness of evil had to be faced. He has been there before us, and by his ultimate victory on the cross has shown us that it is from the darkest place that the deepest healing comes.

SEVENTH SUNDAY BEFORE CHRISTMAS

God's building

> Luke 20.17 (*JB*) *'It was the stone rejected by the builders that became the keystone.'*

Anyone whose childhood memories go back to the dim, flickering images of the early movies might remember being half amused and half alarmed (as young children are by clowning), at the antics of a group of comic policemen. They scrambled and scattered chaotically all over the place, forever chasing but never, it seemed, actually catching their quarry – always isolated from their objective by a series of bizarre misadventures. They were called the 'Keystone Kops' – inaptly, I think, because a keystone is a unifying agent and the kops were anything but unified. They simply had not 'got it together'.

1 *Rhythm and order*

Like so many of the first comedy classics often ending in a futile chase, the films made by the Keystone Company were not calculated to evoke that image of bonding and unity which is the very function of the keystone in architecture. What a tremendous moment it must have been during the building of one of the mighty medieval abbeys, when a major keystone was lowered into place at the summit of an arch - crowning the whole edifice and locking it together. The keystone was, in fact, a potent symbol for the community called to live out its monastic life within the abbey walls. It involved a rhythmic, ordered round, far removed from the frantic disharmony of the comedy cops and their like.

2 *A sense of rejection and futility*

Why, when we watch such chaotic goings-on safely distanced from us, as they are on the screen, do we find ourselves moved to laughter? Is it because the child, deep down, is still half alarmed at the possibility of his own world disintegrating into chaos, and laughter relieves the anxiety? Perhaps we are defending ourselves against the inexpressible sense of rejection that has come down to us from Adam, cast out as he was from the harmony which God had created out of primeval chaos; isolated as he was from God, from creation, even from his wife. We can identify with Adam in those depths of alienation: 'Life', we might say, 'is a futile chase, full of bizarre misadventures'.

And so it might be if it were not for the loving wisdom of the One who identifies with us in our isolation, allowing himself to be exposed to the very depths of forsakenness, that we may never again be forsaken.

3 *The master builder*

So God in his lovingkindness recreates alienated humanity. The analogy frequently found in the Bible for this work of

God is that of building. God is the master builder who crowns his building and holds it all together with the headstone – the keystone – who is Christ. It is in him that the whole work comes to completion. But, whereas the human master builder marks out the choicest part of the quarry, carefully selecting the stone which will be lovingly and skilfully wrought for its place of honour, the one chosen by God for the summit of *his* building is one that has been 'despised and rejected of men'.

4 *Centred on Christ*

The cinema screen has been replaced for most of us by the smaller frame of the TV, but the flickering images still pass across our vision to amuse, to alarm, and to leave us with a sense of unfulfilment. And if we dare to stop and listen to our deepest self we begin to see how our life has been scattered and disintegrated in so many futile ways. What we need is to be gathered up and given back our essential harmony. The way of Christ is the way of creation out of chaos. If we tread that way, centring our lives on him, we shall begin to find in all our relationships, all our work, that there is rich meaning in the true image of the 'keystone', for God is building us into what he wants us to be.

SIXTH SUNDAY BEFORE CHRISTMAS with the SUNDAY NEXT BEFORE ADVENT

An apocalyptic pattern

> Romans 8.35 (*AV*) '*Who shall separate us from the love of Christ? Shall tribulation or distress, or persecution or famine, or nakedness or peril or the sword?*'

1 *Magnificent patchwork*

The centre-piece of a certain rural exhibition of arts and

crafts was a magnificent patchwork quilt, of impressive dimensions and exquisite workmanship. The multicoloured sections had not – as one might have assumed at first glance – been put together haphazardly, but were carefully arranged in a subtle continuity of tone and pattern. Closer inspection revealed particular themes sustained throughout to make an overall design. The quilt was unique of its kind, and clearly marked '*not for sale*'. How could its creator have parted with it when each of the small components was to her a type of memento? Every patch had been cut out from a remnant of clothing or soft furnishing associated with members of her close family. Over the years she had accumulated the materials for a mosaic of remembrance. It was a piece of domestic history embodied in needlework.

2 *A composite product*

The thirteenth chapter of St Mark, sometimes referred to as a 'Little Apocalypse', from which we get the last two gospel readings before Advent, is likewise unique. Nowhere else in the whole of his manuscript does Mark put such a lengthy discourse into the mouth of Jesus. The problem for bible scholars is that parts of it are strangely at odds with the impression of our Lord given by the rest of Mark's work. This chapter appears to resemble the patchwork quilt; a composite product, reminiscent of more than one phase of communal history. It is possible that not every utterance ascribed to Jesus in the passage is authentically his; the evangelist may, for instance, have inserted part of the missionary preaching of the first christian Church. Our first reaction, therefore, might be to undervalue or even discredit the whole passage, until we realize that the themes running through it bear a critical relevance to christian discipleship of every age, including our own.

3 *A mosaic of fact and fiction*

The calamitous effects of internecine strife predicted in these verses have become familiar to us all through the medium of television; the world's catastrophes invade the domestic scene several times a day, as the news bulletins are repeated. The problem for the viewer is that hard news and fiction become jumbled together to produce a bewildering mosaic, in which real-life horrors are followed instantly by television drama, often portraying similar horrors; and the patchwork effect is further heightened by the insertion of advertisements. These commercial persuaders promise a society in which there is no pain or disfigurement. They invite the consumer into a fantasy world, where everyone is happy and beautiful and enjoying the luxury of an ideal home. This mixture is distilled for readers of quality newspapers by the weekend colour supplements. In these they find glossy pages of advertising devoted to the 'good life', interspersed with articles reflecting a hard and often violent world.

4 *Living under an illusion*

Fact and fantasy thus mingled together and issuing from the same source, can exert a deadening influence. They have the power to anaesthetize us against reality. Whereas previous generations constantly experienced the harshnesses of life at first hand, we, in our consumer society, are in danger of living under an illusion of invulnerable security until we come face to face with some personal tragedy. When this happens, how well equipped shall we be to cope with it?

It is vital for christians to be aware of the two great themes woven into the magnificent patchwork of Mark's 'Little Apocalypse', and to invest them with the importance and urgency warranted by the signs of our time.

5 *An alarm bell in a turbulent world*

The injunction to 'Be on your guard' is repeated at intervals throughout the chapter, like the ringing of an alarm bell. It is meant to sound a note of warning to disciples living, as indeed we are, in the midst of a turbulent world where impersonal forces are at work threatening to diminish our sense of individual responsibility and to erode our faith. Let christians beware of the condition characterized by the wars and rumours of wars happening in the world; a condition in which we are tempted to believe that the individual counts for nothing. It is not so, within the purposes of God! Each of us is marked out as unique, and so the quality of each christian life will determine the quality of the Church as a whole, in our small section of its history.

6 *The message of hope*

The second main theme in this apocalyptic pattern is one of comfort. The word is used in its older and deeper sense, derived from the same root as 'fortitude' and 'fortress'. When the woes of the world arrive on the domestic scene as hard and bitter fact rather than fiction, they disclose our personal helplessness. Our first reaction then is to shrink away; to find some way of bypassing the pain and disturbance they bring. It is precisely at this point that the word of reassurance and strength comes to us from the gospel, 'Do not be alarmed . . . with these things the birth pangs of the new age begin'. Whether we hear those words against the clamour and commotion of contemporary history, or the inward turbulence of our own feelings, they carry a message of hope, they mark the difference between a shallow fantasy existence and the deepest reality.

7 *The heart of the gospel*

At the heart of our faith two components are mingled together; pain and love. The excruciating pain of the cross, and the love that, in spite of every human instinct to shrink away from suffering, stayed with it, remaining weak and vulnerable but winning a victory in which we can share. The cup that was offered to Jesus on the cross was of wine mingled with bitter gall. The sparkling wine of obedience to a loving Father and the joy of doing his will, must have intensified the bitterness of the Passion. To those who are not fatalists, living without hope or belief, to those who follow a crucified and risen Jesus, the suffering of the world must seem the greatest tragedy. The apocalyptic message in Mark's gospel is recalling us to the great reality at the centre of our faith, that however much the forces of destruction may invade our world, whatever threatening catastrophe may overtake us individually, God's loving design will in the end prevail and 'nothing shall separate us from the love of God which is in Christ Jesus Our Lord'.[1]

ADVENT SUNDAY

Common humanity

Matthew 25.40 (*NEB*) '*Anything you did for one of my brothers here, however humble, you did for me.*'

1 *Victorian values*

I would like you to picture the words 'THOU SHALT NOT . . . ' beautifully inscribed in gold lettering upon dark wood, or lovingly embroidered on canvas and skilfully framed, or even painstakingly carved out, in fretwork. They are words from the Ten Commandments. In Victorian churches they were set alongside the Creed and the Lord's Prayer and are still to be seen on many a sanctuary wall occupying the conspicuous position accorded to them by the Victorian church.

Imagine yourself sitting in a Barchester pew at Morning Prayer dressed in the starchy uprightness of Sunday 'best'. You are listening to a thunderous sermon full of stern

1. Romans 8.39

moralism and, as you listen, your eye falls upon the prominent 'Thou Shalt Nots' of the Decalogue. You return home and once again your eye is caught; this time by the embroidered text hanging above the fireplace 'Thou O God Seest Me'. You are left in no doubt about your accountability to God and you are made acutely mindful of the theme of his judgement; indeed, of his vengeance, if the sermon has been fiery enough! Some people laugh at outdated Victorian values. Some want them to be reinstated by force, if necessary, before total anarchy sets in. Some, (probably those who make up the well-known 'silent majority') have a haunting awareness that we *ought* to be accountable for our behaviour, but not in any way that leads to neurotic guilt, or, as with more than one Victorian paterfamilias, to hypocrisy.

2 *A standard of judgement*

Yet one of the great themes to be put before us in this season of Advent is the theme of judgement and because, if anything is to be judged, one needs a standard to judge it by, we have to find the right standard, the true criterion of our accountability to God and to society.

If we take on board the notion of a wrathful, vengeful God as portrayed in some of the narrow and distorted forms of religion, then surely our lifestyle will likewise become narrow and distorted; even in some cases to the point of neurosis.

On the other hand, we cannot merely drift irresponsibly into whatever lifestyle happens to come along, and allow it to dictate what we do about such important features of life as marriage, work, money or physical health. Such activities have to be rooted in some sort of firm belief, or they may run riot.

So what is the christian criterion of judgement? How will the line of accountability be drawn?

3 *The gospel of belonging*

I you look up the word for judgement in Greek (Krinein) you will find that it has the basic meaning 'to separate' or 'to divide off', just as the shepherd in Palestine divided up his mixed flock at nightfall; the favoured sheep with their woolly fleeces from the less valuable, yet vulnerable, goats, who needed to be taken inside for warmth. He could detect them easily in the half-light by their colour, the light-coloured fleeces of the sheep contrasting with the darker hides of the goats. But it is not by the criterion of colour that human sheep are to be divided from human goats, or by status, or power, or even religion. The standard is quite simply that of common humanity. We shall be judged, says our Lord, on whether we accepted the obligations of being truly human or not.

Wherever common humanity is denied, not simply by terrorism and violence but by indifference and apathy, then Christ is being denied because he identifies himself with the needy and the underprivileged. 'Anything you do not do for one of these, however humble, you did not do it for me.'

For most of us who are at a distance, mentally or physically, from the storm-centres of danger and oppression in the world, it is not easy to apply our Lord's criterion to ourselves. Yet there is a gospel of belonging which we shall hear again in four weeks time in the Christmas message. It reminds us that man and his whole environment belong to God and that people, being children of the same Father, belong to each other.

Two commandments embrace and sum up all the others; they are not to be found in the frame of ten, for they come later. 'Thou shalt love the Lord thy God with all thy heart, soul, mind and strength' and 'Love thy neighbour as thyself'.

They were given to us by him who was born vulnerable to the pains, insults and total indifference of men. Yet they stand as the ground of our judgement and our hope.

ADVENT 2

The liberating good news

Luke 4.18 (*NEB*) *'He has sent me to announce good news to the poor.'*

1 *Able to receive*

Do any of you remember VJ night? What a night of celebration! The Japanese had surrendered and the war was over. Soon the emaciated inmates of the prison camps would be rejoicing at the good news. And yet, deep in a jungle in New Guinea, a single infantryman soldiered on, imagining himself still to be conducting hostilities under the Nipponese flag. Finally he emerged and they told him that the war was over *and had been for twenty years*! It is hardly credible that he should have been cut off for so long, so isolated that he remained in ignorance for two whole decades. Nevertheless, there he stands as a prime example of someone who was not in a position to receive the vital news. Not everyone is: it's no use telling a cripple that he has just won a skiing holiday, or a deaf man that a wonderful concert is shortly to be arranged. Such news fails to touch their lives any more than VJ night affected the lone infantryman; yet this was the same night that for others – the many Far East prisoners of war – heralded liberation itself. Surely the point is clear: it is necessary to be in the right situation to receive 'good news', otherwise the very phrase loses its meaning.

2 *Knowing the need of God*

In the words of the prophet Isaiah, quoted by Jesus in today's gospel, the 'poor' are they who are to receive the good news. In the Authorized Version the word for them is 'meek'. Either word, however, can sound misleading in today's use of language. Perhaps the nearest we can approach might be to call them the 'unproud', and to find a clue to their identity we can look at our Lord's first beatitude where 'meek' is also re-translated: in a modern version it reads, 'Blessed are they who . . . *know their need of God*'.

To be unaware of the spiritual dimension to life, to exist within a closed round of projects and pleasures without reference to their eternal background – to be in a way like that lone infantryman – is to be cut off from our own deepest needs and from the needs of others. Within the jungle of our habits and prejudices and private defences, the dynamic word of Jesus cannot reach us.

3 *Hearing and rejecting*

The congregation of the synagogue in Jesus' home town of Nazareth had come, as we do, to receive the ministry of the word. They had come, like us, to hear the scriptures read, to join in the prayers, and to hear an address. The setting for their worship was not greatly different from ours, except that whoever preached did so from a chair and not from a pulpit. The one who sat before them to expound the passage of Isaiah that he had chosen as the reading was their contemporary. It is not difficult for us, therefore, to identify with the Nazareth congregation as they listened to the words of Isaiah being read and expounded, for Jesus is also *our* contemporary, and his word is addressed equally to us in the present moment. He still speaks from the prophet that great message of healing and liberation, and he still claims that today, in our very hearing, the prophecy is fulfilled. He is the one who comes to set us free. Those first hearers in his home town rejected him. They were not in a position to receive the good news. Perhaps because they *were* his own people they could not take him 'neat'. The stunning reality of Jesus' message and his mission cut across all their familiar securities: so they threw him out. Shall we continue to identify with them in rejecting the dynamic word that invites us to emerge from whatever is clogging our freedom?

4 *Out of captivity*

It would be fascinating to have been present when the lone soldier emerged after two decades in the jungle, to be told that over all those years he had been living out a fantasy. Was his instant reaction one of joy and relief, or was there – if only for a moment – an instinct to 'cut and run' back into the safety of his hideaway? The word of God as we encounter him in Advent comes as a judgement on our false securities. He comes to set us free from the fantasies that have been sustaining us all these years. He comes to call us out into the open, to dare to expose our weakness, our blindness, our inner captivity – or whatever is hindering the mission and the ministry he longs to exercise through us.

ADVENT 3

An end and a beginning

Matthew 11.10 (*NEB*) '*Here is my herald . . .*'

1 *Dead leaves and new growth*

Hedges of beech or hornbeam stand out at this time of the year against the bareness of the landscape. Clinging tenaciously to their foliage despite the gales of winter, they present a warm and cheerful appearance. They also provide us with a telling symbol for Advent. The leaves, once fresh and green, are now golden brown, attractive to the eye but dead and eventually destined to be cast off to make way for the new growth. A close observer might discern, even now, the tiny undeveloped buds that will form growing points in the spring. Such works of nature contain an end and a beginning. The death-bearing season, signified by the old leaves hanging on in apparent security, must be replaced in a living hedge by the life-bearing season whose promise is already visible. What a striking illustration of the Advent theme with its notes of earnest warning and joyful expectation sounding together.

2 *The watchmen of the Old Testament*

In this season of the Church's year, the readings and prayers of the liturgy challenge us to cast off all that is dry and dead in our lives as christians and to wait in simple trust for the approach of Christ at Christmas who brings, by his coming, the promise of grace and renewal. We share at this time in the experience of those who, long before his nativity, yearned for his coming and prepared for it by their words and deeds as did those great watchmen of the Lord the Old Testament prophets. They march through the history of Israel like so many sandwich-board men bearing placards announcing a forthcoming occasion. Each man's proclamation is couched in a style that is different and distinctive from all the others, yet *all of them are pointing onward to the same event*!

The last and greatest of these arresting figures is John the Baptist. He stands between two ages, embracing by his life and witness the end of the Old Testament and the beginning of the New. He points like his predecessors, towards the saviour who is yet to come, but he is to be distinguished from all the others; for them the day of the Lord was a distant prospect, for him it was close at hand.

3 *Faith in darkness*

There is an old Persian proverb which in translation reads thus; '*A place where the sun always shines is a desert*'. We might add a corollary from the spiritual wisdom of Christendom, that a faith which is able to survive only in the sunshine of certainty, never experiencing the darkness of doubt, is no true faith. The history of John the Baptist testifies to the truth that a strong faith inevitably contains an element of doubt. Having announced, with burning conviction, the imminence of Christ's coming, he found himself cut off physically from the sunlight in the darkness of Herod's prison, and there he was besieged by doubt. He sent some of his most loyal helpers to ask whether or not

Jesus was indeed the expected Christ; they returned with a reply that would inspire and sustain him at his hour of crisis. The answer came, not in the form of a searing and blinding revelation, but as a factual account of the healing actions that signified the presence of a living God.

Advent is a season to remind us how God can come to us in our own darkness. There are times when our anxieties and uncertainties cling on like dead leaves, despite the unmistakeable signs of growth clearly evident as we pause and look back on the distance we have travelled in our faith. At those times of darkness we are sharing in the experience of faithful men and women in every age who, like John in his prison, have been tormented by doubt. Can we, in each crisis of faith, take a positive step as he did to turn in the direction of Christ? It may be that loyal friends can be for us, as they were for John, the messengers of hope to assure us that somewhere God's sunlight of love is still shining in the world. It may even be that we use the occasion of our heart's misgiving to take pencil and paper and to write down the ground of our difficulty, turning it into a prayer which can be prayed repeatedly during the darkness.

The kingdom which John proclaimed with such vigour and conviction has come. That is an evergreen fact which we shall celebrate again this Christmas. In those moments when, by contrast, our own faith seems brown and dead and doubts assail us, let us reflect upon the experience of John the Baptist and know that, in light or in darkness, we never pass out of God's love.

ADVENT 4

Borrowed or blue

Matthew 1.23 (*RSV*) *'Behold a virgin shall conceive and bear a son, and his name shall be called Emmanuel (which means God with us).'*

1 *A wedding rhyme*

Popular folklore is often expressed in verse. Here is a couplet which prescribes the four essentials a bride should wear on her wedding day, in order to bring her luck. . .

Something old, something new,
Something borrowed, something blue.

The origin and meaning of this precept is hard to discover, since it comes out of a verbal and not a written tradition; current opinion, when canvassed, was only forthcoming about the second line of the rhyme. Apparently the article or garment borrowed has to come from someone close to the wife-to-be, a person whose sterling qualities will then somehow rub off on her. If the lender's marriage has been happy, hers will likewise be happy, and so on.

The notion of wearing or carrying something blue follows a similar principle but in a richer and deeper vein, blue being the colour traditionally taken to represent the Virgin Mary. This means, by implication, that in some sense the girl who wears blue is associating herself with the mother of our Lord, the young bride whose first-born son bore the prophetic name Emmanuel, God with us.

So a simple bridal jingle brings us to the climax of today's gospel, and if we change its reference from weddings and apply it to Christmas, we shall find the words of the rhyme strangely appropriate as we approach the forthcoming festival.

There will certainly be something old in close proximity to something new in many homes, where the Victorian Christmas tree is surrounded by micro-computerized electronic games. Sadly, in so many places, the 'something borrowed' will be Christmas itself or the money to pay for it. People will borrow Christ's birthday to celebrate whatever they want to celebrate regardless of its simple message; the lending/spending extravaganza will not be paid for until long after the decorations are down, the empty bottles have been recycled and the expensive toys discarded.

We too often sentimentalize Christmas in the same way that we sentimentalize weddings, spending a lot of money on it and taking it away from the realms of reality into a kind of candy-floss fantasy. The fantasy ends when the honeymoon of Christmas day and Boxing Day are over and we wake up to the everyday world without its make-up on. How do we find ourselves approaching the feast of Christ's nativity in a cruel, violent and divided society? Are we allowing the pressures of the 'borrowed' Christmas to hustle us into eating too much, drinking too much and spending too much, or are we in some sense associating ourselves with those who, like Mary and her baby, are among the poor outcasts and rejects of today's world? If you really want to make some small gesture on Christmas day to mark its true meaning, why not place a gift envelope for the hungry of the world right there on the Christmas dinner table? Like the bride and her 'borrowed blue' we shall then have to return it. We shall be duly enriched by our having used it, because in so doing we have opened ourselves to receive some small part of Mary's qualities of generosity and love.

CHRISTMAS DAY

Fact or fantasy?

John 1.14 (*AV*) *'And the Word was made flesh and dwelt among us.'*

1 *Silent snowfall*

Traditional Victorian Christmas cards, with their evocative pictures of the olden days in town or country, generally have one outstanding feature in common; whatever the setting, it is depicted under a thick blanket of snow. Snow is nature's sound proofing agent, deadening the echo of footsteps on the pavement and muffling the wheels of passing traffic. When it comes at this time of year, it seems to endorse some of the familiar phrases being sung in the carols . . . 'See amid the winter snow, born for us on earth below', 'How silently, how silently, the wondrous gift is given', 'The world in solemn stillness lay to hear the angels sing'.

2 *Crossing a kind of no-man's land*

The mood of the carols is in such sharp contrast to the violence and noisy banalities of the world around us that when the fever of the commercial Christmas is over and the majestic hush of the nativity invites us to worship, we may seem to cross a kind of no-man's land, away from reality. For a brief space we are part of a fantasy (or so it appears), beautiful and evocative like the old-fashioned Christmas card scenes, but having no relevance to real life as we experience it today.

3 *Crossing an actual no-man's land*

How did Christmas appear to those troops from both sides in the First World War who crossed an actual no-man's land on 25 December 1914? For a brief space the big guns were stilled; there was an eerie hush over the battle lines until the silence was broken by the sound of laughter and singing. Germans and British had dared to leave their trenches and were meeting one another, not as enemies, but as fellow human beings. It would be interesting to know how each soldier recalled that brief encounter once the bombardment and the slaughter had been resumed.[1] Was it passed off as a momentary illusion or did it stay in the mind and heart as a reality strong enough to give grounds for hope? Was it fact or fantasy that the short-lived Christmas celebration represented?

4 *Our own response to Emmanuel*

Their answer to that question belongs now to history. Ours will be required of us – albeit in a different context – within a few days when the tree, the lights, the warmly-worded greetings-cards and all the other visible signs of celebration have been tidied away. Then we shall discover whether he whose birth we celebrate today lives beyond today in our minds and hearts, or whether we have allowed the artificial snowfall of a fantasy 'white Christmas' to obscure the continuing reality of Emmanuel: 'God-with-us'.

5 *The ongoing encounter*

The setting for the birth of God into the world of men is one of simplicity and peace; no sound of human speech is recorded as having broken the solemn stillness of the stable. The word was made flesh against a background of silence 'the silence of eternity interpreted by love.'[2] Those who came to his manger-cradle were there to offer their gifts, to adore and to perceive for one glorious moment that reality which still stands out against a world of darkness and illusion and cannot be overcome by it.

1. It is shameful to recall that, following this incident, fraternization with the enemy was forbidden on pain of death.
2. From the hymn 'Dear Lord and Father of mankind', John Whittier, 1807–92.

We have come to church today to re-enact that moment of tranquil worship. It cannot be dismissed as a passing fantasy, for it is the beginning of an ongoing encounter between God and man. The silence of the stable will be followed by the solemn hush around the darkening cross and the awesome stillness of the tomb. Our Lord calls us to share each experience and, with him, to reach beyond them all to the promise of resurrection. Here is a reality strong enough to give grounds of hope to a world fragmented by its pains and pleasures, and desperately needing the grace and truth of Christmas.

SUNDAY AFTER CHRISTMAS

Letting go and moving on

Luke 2.29 (*JB*) '*Now Master you can let your servant go in peace.*'

The words of an old man holding a baby in his arms; a situation common enough for us to make a number of mental pictures from familiar experience.

A grandfather sitting in his favourite chair nursing the latest grandchild; a not so young vicar cradling an infant at the baptismal font; a department-store Father Christmas lifting up the smallest child in the queue the better to hear her whispered request; the images come easily to the mind, each reminding us of the unique bond often existing between very young children and the elderly, between the little ones who have not yet shouldered the burden of worldly cares or ambitions and the old ones who have been through it all and have come out on the other side with dignity.

1 *The desolation of old age*

Or have they? That part of the scenario does not always ring true. How many of them arrive at retirement age and beyond, disappointed in their early hopes, feeling desperately unfulfilled, and thus finding old age a time of bitterness and disillusionment? Coming to terms with diminishment and loss of status, and coping with failing powers in ourselves and others; these are among the most testing situations we ever encounter. They come to most of us late on in life, accompanied not infrequently by physical illness. The desolation that can threaten old age is given an air of finality in such expressions as 'past it' or 'over the hill' by the language of a society which idolizes youth and vigour.

2 *God coming into the situation*

But we cannot regard the old, nor must they regard themselves, as somehow 'over', like a vase of withered flowers. For them there has to be a coming to terms with the past, a letting go and a moving forward. There *is* an answer to their predicament and it can be found in the response of the holy old man Simeon to a six-week-old baby.

Most casual observers, looking at the crowds of visitors entering the temple, would hardly have spared a second glance for a working-class couple with their child, but Simeon's eyes were enlightened. He had been waiting and watching for this moment and now it had come in a way that he could never have predicted. He saw, in that infant, God coming into the situation, and he knew that when God comes in, the situation is transformed. The great painter, John Constable, is said to have once been watching a child attempting to paint a landscape. As he saw her becoming more and more frustrated with her own efforts, he stepped in and, borrowing the brush, made a few swift strokes on the canvas. Nothing of what she had done was altered but the whole picture was transformed.

To all those who are frustrated by the changes and chances of a fleeting world, especially to the ones who in later life feel caught in a pattern of decline, the response of Simeon shows a way forward. Wait and watch for God in your situation; consciously prepare for his coming. Wait and watch in childlike simplicity with faith and trust, remembering the old man with the infant Christ in his arms, and learning from that gospel picture three things: first, to come to terms, at whatever stage in life, with what we are and who we are; 'Yes Lord, this is where I am at in life. These are my strengths and weaknesses. This is the situation that is causing me pain, anxiety, and, sometimes, anger. Come into that situation and help me to see it by your light; the light of eternity.'

Second, to learn from the one who had waited so long for God's promise, that whoever we are and whatever we are, God wants a special thing from each of us, something that no one else can do; part of his plan for us that was there before we were born. He has not made us for nothing but for a purpose. Father Damian Lundy FSC is an experienced conductor of retreats for young people from all walks of life. For those who come, haunted by the fear of failure or uselessness, he has a slogan: 'Say to yourself, "I'm not junk. I'm O.K. 'cos God don't make junk; he collects it!".'

Thirdly, from Simeon, that great watchman of the Lord, we must learn (before we are summoned to our own personal Nunc Dimittis) to look again at those features of life to which we are giving most of our time and attention. It may be that some of the things we are hanging on to will have to be shed in order that life may be simplified. It may be that this is the time to move forward into a new awareness of God and of that unique bond which exists between him and each one of his children.

EPIPHANY

The giver and the gift

> Matthew 2.11 (*RSV*) '. . . *they fell down and worshipped him. Then opening their treasures they offered him gifts. . .*'

1 *Money in lieu*

Among the recent crop of cards and letters delivered in the Christmas mail, a number will have included, along with the sender's seasonal greetings, a message that might have read something like this: 'Dear . . . I was at a loss for a suitable present to give you so this year I am sending money in lieu.' Also enclosed, the recipient would have discovered a cheque or money-order for an amount partly intended to salve the donor's conscience, and therefore liable to be viewed secretly by both parties as somewhat over-generous. The person on the receiving end may have experienced a mixed reaction. Such a lavish sum could admittedly be put to good use but somehow it is not the same as a more tangible – if less extravagant – present, wrapped and labelled and waiting to be opened on Christmas day. A mere cheque, whatever the figure shown on its face, hardly seems to carry the same promise or to establish the same bond with the giver, as a gift in kind. Imagine the Magi journeying over moor and mountain in order to bring the Christ-child a cheque drawn on some Eastern bank!

2 *The bond of giving*

Today's gospel tells us that the travellers *opened* their treasures; they observed, as we do, the preliminary ritual of unwrapping and revealing the hidden gifts. What they brought out were rich and costly things, gold, frankincense and myrrh, totally unsuitable – as we would think – for a small baby, yet bearing a promise and establishing a bond which all the cunning and cruelty of Herod could not break. The very earliest representations of the Epiphany show Mary holding up the child and presenting him to the gentile strangers, thus revealing, in response to their homage, the divine gift being given to the world. When we give presents to our near and dear ones, there is a deep sense in which what is written on the miniature label attached to the outside wrapping, is as important as the gift inside: 'To . . . with all my love and gratitude': words that together with the tangible shape and content of the gift, enrich and deepen the bond between us.

3 *Weddings and worship*

Think of the bond between husband and wife, married long enough ago to have had no option at the time of their wedding but to use the words of the Book of Common Prayer. As he bound his bride to him with the gift of a ring, the groom would have made this solemn pledge: 'With my body I thee worship and with all my worldly goods I thee endow.' There are some who regret the loss of the word 'worship' from the more modern version of the marriage vows in the Alternate Service Book. Others welcome the mutuality in the newer service whereby the bride is no longer a passive recipient but may herself offer a ring and respond in words identical to those used by the bridegroom. Both points of view are valid. Together they affirm for us one of the great truths of Epiphany, that genuine giving implies profound interdependence which, at its best, involves – as it did with the Magi – an element of worship. When we offer our gifts in sincerity and love, they convey a message transcending what is written on the label. Its meaning – although it is not to be recorded in words – might read something like this: 'Dear . . . This gift may not be suitable but it is sent in acknowledgement of your wor[th]ship to me and mine to you. Therefore it is part of that oneness in Christ in whose worship and love we find our deepest bond.'

We have come to worship at Epiphany following in the steps of the Magi, to make our own offering; to present all that we have and all that we are to Christ. He gives us in return the gift of himself and in that living bond with the risen Lord we find the mutual love we are called to convey to the world.

FIRST SUNDAY AFTER EPIPHANY

Part with Him

John 1.29 (*NEB*) *'Look, there is the Lamb of God that takes away the sin of the world.'*

1 *Signs of the festive season*

Whilst the January sales have long since banished from the shops all traces of the recent festive season, the Church calendar reveals that we are still in the period of Epiphany. A season which began with the celebration of royal gifts and giving at the coming of the Magi.

Whilst the post-Christmas house cleaning will likewise have, days ago, removed any such signs of festivity as decorations, Christmas cards and the remnants of wrapping paper, the presents that came gift-wrapped (unless they were instantly consumed) are still somewhere in evidence. It is worth a moment's reflection upon where they are and what might have happened to them. If they were of a highly practical kind they may now be part of the household equipment; if decorative or ornamental, part of the wardrobe or the display cabinet. If edible they may already in an indirect way have become physically part of the recipient!

Excluding complimentary business hand-outs and the sort of presents that are given from a reluctant sense of duty, it is likely that the givers gave to the choosing of their gifts a real measure of care and sacrifice. Thus the giver is part of the gift, the gift becomes part of the one who receives it and, thereby, a bond is established between them.

The same truth is expressed in every meal which is not merely a business formality or an occasion of polite but reluctant duty, but is based on genuinely mutual giving and receiving.

2 *A common meal in the classroom*

There was a certain lecturer at a College of higher education, who gave adult evening classes in *Cordon bleu* cookery. At the end of each weekly two-hour session a delicious dish would have been produced. One evening the class decided that, instead of drawing lots to decide who should take home the *plat du jour*, they would sample it there and then in the classroom. The simple act of eating together in what had hitherto been an environment of formal instruction, gave rise to such a warmth of fellowship that they repeated the experience the following week. On the third occasion one student shyly produced a table cloth. Several desks were pushed together. Knives and forks appeared as if from nowhere and a tradition was begun. From then on, each weekly class was followed by a brief but cordial communal meal. Food that had been regarded as a lecture-room specimen took on a deeper significance. It became a gift, an essential part of the life of the group. The lecturer subsequently reported that the cookery course, so far from being harmed by this development, had been enriched and transformed. The members had found a new common identity because they were enabled by that shared gift, to be more fully themselves.

3 *Primitive sacrificial meals*

There, in an urban classroom in the twentieth century, was a link with the primitive religious practice from which the

Jewish Passover developed: the establishing of kinship by a common meal. Among nomadic tribes in ancient times one of the highest gifts that could be offered to God or man would have been a lamb. It became the basis of a sacrificial meal, a holy offering, the entire animal being consumed at the time of the meal and none of it kept for private consumption later.

4 *Christians part of the Lamb*

The age-old bond of shared food is expressed and celebrated most fully in the Christian Eucharist. Christ allowed himself to become the sacrificial Lamb, the basis of this holy meal in which he himself is a gift to us and becomes part of us. He calls each Christian sent out from his altar, to become an expression of his love, with all the care and sacrifice that it entails. Let us by our kinship with him face the encounters which lie before us in the coming days, determined not to allow disappointment to harm or diminish our relationships. In so doing we shall become mysteriously with Christ, a part of the holy Lamb of God that takes away the sin of the world.

SECOND SUNDAY AFTER EPIPHANY

At home with the Gospel

John 1.39 (*NEB*) '*They went and saw where he was staying.*'

1 *The electronic home*

An eventual outcome of the rapid advances being made by computer technology, will be the re-emergence of the home as a fundamental unit of society. This is the view expressed by a leading observer[1] of what has been called 'the communications revolution' in which electronics are replacing print as a basic medium of information. He foresees a not too distant future when easy access to computer links will make it possible for daily work, education and various forms of communal decision making, to be done entirely within the home environment.

2 *No settled home*

Contrast this profile of the twenty-first century with the first century environment in which Jesus carried on his ministry, having – once he had left Nazareth – no settled home of his own. The Gospels show his work of teaching, healing and feeding, being done for the most part, in public places and usually in the open air. He himself is recorded as saying '*Foxes have holes and the birds of the air have nests but the Son of Man has nowhere to lay his head.*[2]

3 *Domestic hospitality*

Occasionally however, the veil is lifted from his personal life and we find him, as at Bethany and at Cana of Galilee, in a domestic environment. Today's Gospel reading from St John hints at a lodging, some place of retreat to which he could invite visitors; a threshold that might be crossed to meet him in private.

It was within this homely context that his first disciples were drawn to him. The Gospel is quite specific about the time of day when it happened. *It was then*, says the Evangelist, *about four in the afternoon*; neither during the rush of a working morning, nor during the torpor in the middle of the day, but in the late afternoon when the mood was appropriate to domestic hospitality.

1. Alvin Toffler *The Third Wave*, Collins, 1985.
2. Luke 9.58.

4 *'Come and see'*

The first word of Jesus in the Fourth Gospel is a question addressed to these potential followers who are waiting upon him. He asks them what they are looking for. Their as yet unspoken hope is to learn all they can from one who, at that stage, they take to be no other than a wandering rabbi. Therefore in order to arrange an interview, they respond with a counter question. 'Where are you staying?' Our Lord's reply has a double significance. It takes the conventional form used by a rabbi to draw attention to some new truth. 'Come and see.' St John in his Gospel has two words for 'see'; one to mean physical sight, the other spiritual vision. It is the latter that is used now. They are being invited to discover more than just a temporary location. He is bidding them to explore through him, the inconceivable richness of God's Kingdom. The Gospel tells us that they crossed his threshold and stayed with him for the rest of the day at his lodging, finding in its homely atmosphere that discipleship means nothing less than abiding with him eternally.

5 *Adapting to the future*

If and when the rapidly approaching electronic future brings people to live and work together in greater and more constant proximity, the challenge to Christian discipleship will be unavoidable. There will be a need – more urgent than ever before – to find ways of bringing the faith into touch with day-to-day relationships within the home. Without the insights of the Gospel, the radical changes envisaged could have a disastrous effect upon family and community life. The ghetto mentality and the unwillingness to adapt to new ways which have too often been the experience of churches in every tradition, will have no contribution to make. The implications of it all are both frightening and exciting and it is not easy to see the way forward. It may be that Christians of all denominations must initiate a communications revolution of their own to bring the proclamation of their faith back from its present marginalized slot in the television schedules and into prime time. It may be that with one voice they will find themselves protesting against things appearing on the domestic screens that are morally desensitizing. It may be that in the greater freedom and leisure afforded by the service of computerized robots, there will be time for lingering hospitality and fellowship, so that Christians may say to their neighbours seeking a faith to live by: 'Come and see.'

Whatever the future may bring, present-day Christians like those first disciples, will have an ever deeper need to wait upon Christ who is the same yesterday, today, and for ever.

EPIPHANY 3

The feeding of the disciples

> John 6.56 (*NEB*) '*Where are we to buy bread to feed these people?*'

1 *Efficiency and sufficiency*

Many an amateur boat-builder must have felt some affinity with Noah and his ark as he looked forward to the critical moment when his vessel would be launched. His skill and craftsmanship patiently applied over many months must then be committed to the upholding power of the water. All that efficiency interpreted and fulfilled by the sufficiency of the element for which it was destined. Efficiency, the power to build a boat; sufficiency, the power of the water to float it; the two are complementary.

In today's gospel we find efficiency shown in the power to organize five thousand hungry people, seating them in orderly fashion and organizing systems of food distribution and waste collection. We also find sufficiency revealed in the power to feed them from slender resources and to meet a deeper hunger than the need for physical nourishment alone. The parable might well have been subtitled 'The feeding of the twelve', for in it we see the efficiency of the disciples in dependence upon the sufficiency of Jesus.

2 *Corporate discipleship*

Let us project ourselves into the situation as if we were one of his disciples there on the hillside close to him, being used by him, actually involved at first hand in the work of the Kingdom. Hear him speaking to us, 'Come now, we must feed these people. Let's get organized, what resources have we?' He is exposing us to our own inadequacy and yet drawing us into an experience of commitment to the common task. We are being led to appreciate that our sufficiency is of him. We are his close friends to whom he interprets the events and experiences of life and through whom he seeks to bring in the Kingdom.

3 *Aggregation or congregation?*

In the Church of yesterday it was not easy to practise this corporate discipleship because active ministry was restricted to the professional minority – the clergy – whilst the remaining majority – the laity – passively attended services and 'supported' the clergy as best they could in marginal ways. The local church tended to be an aggregation rather than a congregation. Nowadays things are different!

4 *Stewardship of resources*

There are resources to be used efficiently for him: time, money, physical energy, material possessions, intelligence, and all of it against the background of the tremendous spiritual resources of prayer and silence. 'What resources have we?' he asks us. What resources to feed to serve and to redeem our society? And he will want to know how efficiently we have used those resources. He will demand an account of our stewardship: 'What have you done with *my* food stocks, *my* fuel and atomic power, *my* time, *my* wealth, *my* children?'

5 *We are nothing of ourselves*

It is a demand that exposes us to our weakness and yet draws us into deeper discipleship, knowing that we have nothing but what we draw from Christ. Consider the small child who is totally dependent on Daddy, but when Daddy's birthday comes along they rejoice together in the present that the child has given his father. And that rejoicing is heightened, not diminished by, the knowledge that the gift was bought out of money that came from Dad in the first place! Likewise we are nothing of ourselves. Our sufficiency is of God. What can we honestly claim as our own, other than the fact that he died for us?

As christian communicants we receive bread at the altar which feeds us in a profound way, nourishing us with more than physical nourishment alone. As christian stewards we are called to manifest to the world the love that is seen in Jesus Christ, and to do that we need all the patience and skill of the boat-builder in making practical use of the resources we have been given.

If you consider the feeding miracle through the eyes of a disciple who is deeply concerned to further the Kingdom, you will find yourself wanting to be as efficient as you can in the way you dispose of your time, your abilities, your money and all your other resources, knowing that there are many multiples of five thousand in whom there is a deeper than physical hunger, waiting to be fed.

EPIPHANY 6

The essential goodness of Creation

Matthew 5.48 (*RSV*) '*You must be perfect.*'

1 *Perfect porcelain*

An advertisement in one of the weekend colour supplements carried a half-page picture of a pair of exquisitely designed dinner plates; quality products from a famous porcelain manufacturer. One of them would sell abroad, the other was a casualty. The final inspection had revealed a flaw, invisible to anyone but a specialist, but enough to turn an export into a reject. Something had gone wrong with this particular item during a process that was started from a uniform batch of raw material. It seems that at no point along the production line until the final stage, could the defective plate have been withdrawn, and even then it required the discerning eye and sensitive touch of an expert to distinguish between two apparently identical products. The colour advertisement was commissioned not by the manufacturers, but by a computer company whose monitoring services enabled the firm to reach ever higher standards of excellence. Their aim was to trace and eliminate every possible fault; in short, to achieve perfection.

2 *A promise rather than a command*

There is a Greek word *Teleios*, translated in English as 'perfect', which chimes in with the aim of the porcelain makers because it is used to describe an end product, something that has either reached completion like the factory's finished article, or is mature and fully grown like a ripened crop ready for harvesting. In Matthew's gospel it is used by Jesus when he says to his followers 'You must be perfect'.

As we hear this saying of our Lord, we need to understand that it contains a positive and not a negative ideal.

Perfectionism translated into the sphere of religion is fraught with psychological and spiritual dangers. Aiming at a computerized perfection by concentrating on one's own faults or the faults of others, will result in a travesty of the wholeness and integrity that the Lord intends for each one of us. Certain members of a religious order with an especially austere rule were accustomed in former times to carry an abacus in an inside pocket, snapping a bead along the wire for every occasion of personal besetting sin. In that way they aimed to tot up and compare each day's tally of faults!

The perfection to which our Lord calls us is of a different order; it is not so much concerned with the absence of flaws and blemishes, as with the presence of love and goodness. His words contain a promise rather than a command, which can only be fulfilled as we stop interpreting life in terms of 'I' the achiever, and open ourselves to God the giver. The question to be asked at the end of each day is not 'what have I done?' but, 'What is God doing in me?'

3 *Two spotlights*

There are some striking parallels to be drawn between the making of dinner plates and the process described in the parable of the wheat and the weeds in today's gospel. Let us throw a spotlight on just two of them.

First, both begin with basic raw material – the clay or the seed – *which is potentially good*, reminding us of the essential goodness of God's creation. How difficult it is to hold on to that idea in a world so far fallen into ugliness, violence and greed. The temptation to lose hope is overwhelming unless, like Julian of Norwich, we keep company every step of the way with 'our courteous Lord'. We hear her words about creation coming to us across the centuries, yet timeless in their truth: 'God made it . . . God loves it . . . God keeps it'. She insisted, in spite of intense suffering, that the truth proclaimed in Genesis is eternal: 'God saw everything that he had made and behold it was very good'. (1.31 *AV*)

The second spotlight falls upon the respective processes

of manufacture and growth. Each must continue uninterrupted until the final stage; the products of both factory and field appear identical until the time comes for the expert to make his assessment. The late Father Christopher Bryant, a wise and holy monk, said, 'Only God has the wisdom and power to sift the bad from the good and to liberate the good imprisoned in the bad.'[1]

May our courteous Lord give us the faith and patience to co-operate with his loving will and to leave the judging to him.

NINTH SUNDAY BEFORE EASTER

A parable of hope

Luke 8.4 (*RSV*) '*A Sower went out to sow his seed.*'

1 *Primitive ploughmen*

Here is a piece of rustic folklore from a bygone age, still said or sung by an older generation of countrymen;

Four beans in a row
One for the rook
One for the crow
One to rot and one to grow.

Was it a dirge or a rhapsody? Was it a pessimist's lament that only a fourth part of the seed would escape the depredations of the birds and the mildew; or could it have been the Te Deum of an optimist based on the sure and certain hope that, despite all the hazards, there would be a harvest? If the former, there is far less reason for despondency today. In countries like ours, where the soil is rich and advances in agricultural science have reduced the risk of failure, the proportion of the germinating seed is likely to treble the gloomy prediction of the folksong.

1. *Sunday Meditations* (SPCK, 1968), p.12.

Nowadays, only two square yards of good wheat land are needed to produce a loaf of bread. We do well to remember however, that in much of the world where the soil is poor and farming methods primitive, it is an *inverse* proportion of acreage to production that is likely to be trebled. There are village communities in eastern lands still dependent on ancient ways of husbandry. The peasant farmer, having first sown by hand, patiently plods behind his narrow, ox-drawn plough, to turn the seed into the ground. One Christian Aid worker quoted the incredible statistic of a hundred miles as the distance covered by the primitive ploughman in cultivating just one acre with a scratch plough!

2 *The harvest abundant despite setbacks*

Jesus said in a parable which links us with that patient village husbandman. 'A sower went out to sow his seed and as he sowed some fell along the path and was trodden under foot and the birds of the air devoured it' (one for the rook and one for the crow!). Is that a parable of hope or disillusionment? Is it properly entitled 'the Sower', having in mind his patient endurance in the face of natural hazard, or must we face up to an evident alternative and call it the parable of four samples of soil, three of which, in the end, produced nothing? If, as most commentators believe, our Lord was following popular story-telling tradition and laying the greatest stress upon the end of the narrative, the message we are meant to take from it is about the abundant harvest reaped in spite of inevitable setbacks.

3 *Undefeated love*

In terms of the Kingdom of God, therefore, this is a parable of hope and comfort; but 'comfort' in the biblical sense of the word, that is the ability to endure and to react creatively to the threat of affliction or failure. The progress of the Kingdom is not, like that of a steamroller or a military tank, subjugating by force all that lies in its path. It encounters opposition and is exposed to adversity, a proportion of its endeavour will never succeed, but in the end there will be a harvest because the last word lies with inexhaustible love. What a fragile, vulnerable thing is the seed of faith sown in the soil of our hearts. Susceptible to the rooks and crows of cynicism and disillusionment, in danger of rotting away and never getting down to the root-growth of our personality. Fragile, yes; but give God's comforting Spirit the space for the seed of his love to germinate, and you will see how the last line of the famous old hymn could come true, 'Thy Kingdom stands and grows for ever, till all thy creatures own thy sway.'[1]

EIGHTH SUNDAY BEFORE EASTER

Christ: communicator, interpreter, healer

> Mark 7.37 (*NEB*) '. . . *he even makes the deaf hear and the dumb speak.*'

The practice of 'image' making is not a modern phenomenon, it has merely been intensified by modern techniques of communication. Attempts have always been made to mould opinions and beliefs about some public figure by presenting him or her in a particular light. Each of the four Evangelists, by his selection and arrangement of the material at his disposal, puts before his readers a different image of our Lord. Mark's gospel is the simplest and the earliest, providing a resource for the others to draw upon; but when they come to consider Mark's account of the healing of the deaf man with an impediment in his speech, they all – apparently with deliberate intent – omit it from their own narratives. Why? Was it because they reckoned it to be damaging to Jesus' image? Did they believe that it cheapened him by putting him on a par with all the itinerant

1. 'The day thou gavest', John Ellerton, 1826–93.

wonder-workers and exorcists of his time? Mark's description of the miracle certainly follows a distinctive sequence which closely resembles the quasi-magical healing methods in common use in the ancient world: Jesus took the man aside away from the crowd, put his fingers into his ears, spat and touched his tongue, then, looking up to heaven, he sighed and said 'Ephphatha'.

The signs and gestures culminating in the word of command, even in terms of modern-day entertainment, sound remarkably like the routine of a stage magician. But what a loss it will be to us if we pass over this story without endeavouring to understand what those actions meant to the handicapped patient, and what they might mean to us.

1 *Jesus took the man aside away from the crowd*

The sensitive hospital consultant wishing to make an individual examination on an open ward, without any other staff in attendance, will ask for the curtains to be drawn around his patient's bed to give a measure of privacy. Within that flimsy barrier the examinee is spared embarrassment, personal contact can be established, and in the security of the one-to-one encounter, the frankness and openness which is part of the healing process is encouraged. It is in person-to-person relationships that we grow; without them we are isolated and estranged, like a deaf-mute lost in the noisy crowd. How liberating it can be when the representatives of impersonal authority show a human face to clients or customers, giving each one individual attention. It is not an aloof and impersonal God with whom we have to deal but one who longs to liberate and heal us. If that is to happen, there must be times when we give him our undivided attention, allowing him to take us aside as he took the deaf, stammering man in Mark's gospel. When all the necessary noise and activity of daily life is barriered off, it does *not* mean that we shut off any part of ourselves from him; it *does* mean that in that personal moment we are uniquely open to his action and his word.

2 *Put his fingers into his ears*

'*. . . the communicator to deaf people must be more than a translator – he must also be an interpreter.*'

This is a quotation from a guidebook for those conducting worship for the deaf.[1] It goes on to emphasize the importance of the interpreter's hands in conveying the meaning of what is being said and done. The basic problem of the man in the gospel was deafness. Men and women whose hearing is severely impaired have great difficulty in acquiring intelligible speech; actions quite literally speak louder than words; which is why the patient felt the fingers of Jesus boring into his ears to show that the stoppage was being cleared away. Isaiah's prophetic vision of the new age when 'the ears of the deaf shall be unstopped'[2] was being fulfilled. Whenever, in our own day, ears are opened so that the appeal 'to serve Christ in one another, and love as he loves us'[3] results in compassionate action, we see a glimpse of that new age.

3 *Spat and touched his tongue*

There is potent symbolism in Christ's action; it carries two meanings. The spittle would have been regarded by his contemporaries as an agent of healing, but it also had a sacramental significance, whereby an intimate part of himself was being given and received: 'He is the very spit of his father' we say, meaning that the inherited personal characteristics are there for all to see. It is a wonderful experience to meet a christian who has allowed the Lord's tongue to heal his tongue so that we can truly say of him 'He is the very spit of Christ'.

1. *A Guidebook for those Conducting Divine Worship for Deaf People*, produced for the Church of England Council for the Deaf by the Church Information Office, 1978.

2. Isaiah, Chapter 35, verse 5 (*AV*).

3. *The Alternate Service Book*, Order for Holy Communion Rite A, p.125.

4 *Then looking up to heaven, he sighed, and said to him, 'Ephphatha'*

The word of release spoken after a deep sigh or groan: a desperate heart-rending sound, the cry of God sharing man's sorrow, totally involved with the sufferer in his weakness, telling us that the Lord is never closer to us than in our pains and losses. And then the liberating word, so precious to the Church in every age that it has come down to us in the language in which it was uttered, *Ephphatha*, the climax of that hallowed moment away from the crowd in which something both gentle and powerful happened to the deaf and stammering man. Which of us, among the multitudinous contacts of daily life, does not need his word of liberation and power? The secret of that power is not magic, but love.

SEVENTH SUNDAY BEFORE EASTER

Legalism or liberation

John 8.6 '*Jesus bent down and wrote with his finger on the ground.*'

1 *A walk on the shore*

Let us, in imagination, take a stroll along some secluded beach at low tide. The sea has fallen back to expose a wide stretch of smooth sand, firm enough underfoot for comfortable walking. The unbroken surface also provides a natural etching plate on which we can inscribe our names with bold Picasso-like strokes, using the tip of a walking stick as a stylus. To register one's identity in this way is curiously satisfying. There it is writ large for all to see, displaying, for the time being, an air of permanence as if it were engraved in stone rather than sand. Alas, it has no lasting quality; the incoming tide will soon sweep over it and the record will be lost. In twelve hours' time, when the waves recede again, the unbroken surface will show no trace.

2 *An impermanent record*

The word in New Testament Greek for the process of writing with an incisive instrument upon a smooth surface, as if with the point of a stick in the sand, is *katagraphen*; the dictionary tells us that it carries a secondary meaning 'to register'. The same word is used in today's gospel to describe the action of Jesus in bending down to write – as one translator has it – 'with his finger in the dust upon the ground'.[1] Whatever it was that Jesus wrote was destined, surely, to be obliterated. Anyone who desired to leave a permanent record would hardly inscribe it in such an ephemeral medium as dust or sand. This mysterious gesture of our Lord seems to speak of impermanence; of allowing the register, such as it was, to be blotted out. What might it be saying to us as we approach the beginning of the Lenten season?

3 *He knows that we are but dust*

First, we need to recall the background to Christ's prophetic action; the malice revealed in the hectoring tone of the Pharisees seeking to set a trap for him, and their excessive concern with the letter of the law, blinding them to their own nature. In response to their heartless treatment of the woman whom they are accusing of adultery, Jesus stooped to make a mark in the dust, the symbol of their physical mortality. 'Remember man that you are dust and to dust you shall return.' The liturgy of Ash Wednesday,[2] echoing the story of the Fall, brings home to us the truth the

1. J.B. Phillips, *The New Testament in Modern English*, 1960.

2. See 'Lent, Holy Week and Easter', *Services and Prayers commended by the House of Bishops* (Church House Publishing, CUP and SPCK, 1984), p.26.

self-righteous Pharisees had failed to see, that conviction is designed to lead to repentance. The cross of ashes received by some worshippers on the forehead is a sign of the same truth. It recalls them to their status with God as sinners in need of forgiveness. It is meant to turn them away from false pride towards an awareness of their human frailty. 'Who then to frail mortality shall trust, But limns the water or, but writes in dust', says Francis Bacon.[3] Reflection upon our weakness will lead us to face the truth of our creatureliness. May the beginning of Lent herald six weeks of honesty with ourselves, and a deepening penitence before God.

4 *Judgement and dismissal*

There is a well-worn joke still occasionally used in situation comedies with a courtroom setting about the learned judge who claims to be utterly exhausted. When asked the cause of this extreme fatigue he replies, 'You see, I've been sitting all day!' The humour plays upon the fact that the formal posture from which to deliver a verdict is sitting down. Popes and professors likewise have their seats of authority. In the incident described in the gospel, Jesus had quite deliberately taken his seat, as any other rabbi would when pronouncing judgement, but when pressed to confirm the cruel sentence already passed by the woman's accusers he stooped and scribbled in the dust. It was an arresting action, both judgemental and dismissive. The accusers, not the accused, were to come under judgement, and their legalistic stratagems brought to nothing. The whole episode ends, as we heard, not with the condemnation of the woman, but with her liberation.

How like the 'doodling' we see our children do, is Jesus' scribbling in the dust! We give them 'magic slates' framing a smooth plastic surface on which they make marks with a wooden stylus; then, with a snap of the shutter inside, the whole surface is made clean again. The fact that sin may be

3. From *The World*, Francis Bacon (1561–1626).

forgiven and blotted out is a message for our guilty hearts as we prepare for the season of preparation for Easter. The story does not imply that the woman's sin was treated lightly; neither is it so with us. But as we enter during Lent into a deeper relationship with Jesus, we shall find, as surely the woman did, that his love and our sin are irreconcilable.

Let us, during our imaginary walk along the beach at low tide, before we turn for home lift our heads from the surface of the sand to the horizon and allow the words of a psalm to quicken our vision and renew in us an attitude of service and love . . . 'For look how high the heaven is in comparison of the earth: so great is his mercy also toward those that fear him. Look how wise also the east is from the west so far hath he set our sins from us.'[4]

ASH WEDNESDAY

The perfect model

Luke 18.10 (*NEB*) '*Two men went up to the temple to pray.*'

1 *Whiter than white*

Manufacturers of soap powders and detergents have always made extravagant claims concerning the beneficial effects of their products upon the weekly wash. Nowadays, to judge by their current advertising, they are concerned with enhancing the texture rather than the colour of the garments to be laundered. For several years, however, they were obsessed with achieving surpassing brilliance in all the white materials that went into the nation's washing machines. One brand, its makers declared, had brought Mrs X's sheets to a degree of whiteness which could only be described as 'dazzling', whilst a rival brand proclaimed that Mrs Y's

4. Psalm 103, verses 11 and 12.

sheets were 'whiter than white'. Ah! but let either Mrs X or Mrs Y hang out their sheets on the garden clothes-line against the background of a fresh fall of snow. Then they will discover that all the graphic images of the advertisers are put into a different perspective by comparison with the purity and intense brilliance of nature. Set beside the whiteness of snowflakes, their linen will seem almost grey. In the same way, the brightness of a coal fire in the domestic hearth looks tawdry when the light of the sun strikes directly upon it. It all depends upon the model that one uses for comparison.

2 *An 'unco guid' man*

The second of the gospels set for Ash Wednesday tells us in a parable that two men went into the temple to pray. They did not sit or kneel, as christians in their personal prayers are wont to do, but stood and prayed aloud after the custom of the jews. One of them, a Pharisee, and therefore a scrupulous upholder of traditional Judaism, compared himself with other men far less worthy than he; robbers, swindlers and adulterers. 'Thank God I am not like them; in all conscience I can claim that I have faithfully discharged the duties of my religion.' These were his sentiments, and as far as they went, who could fault them? He was the kind of man who, in the Scottish vernacular, would be referred to a *unco guid* or, to adopt one of the epithets of the soap powder salesmen, he was 'whiter than white' according to the standards of a pious Pharisee.

3 *Searing self-discovery*

The other man, an unlikely visitor to the temple, is described as a tax-gatherer. If he had followed the ways of worldliness and sharp practice generally associated with his class – as surely we are meant to infer – then, in moral and spiritual terms, his life was badly soiled. But in a searing moment of self-awareness, he showed himself ready to face the truth of his condition and to throw himself upon the infinite compassion of God. There was no question of his looking down upon others; 'Who am I to stand before the majesty, the purity and dazzling holiness of God?' Those were *his* sentiments, and as he saw himself over against the divine model, the comparison stirred his heart. Who was it that once said, 'When your heart is stirred you speak in telegrams'? This man's prayer, like a telex message, was short and to the point: 'O God have mercy on me, sinner that I am.'

4 *Lent and new growth*

Why, on this particular day in the Church's year, should the lectionary offer us this cameo of two men; the one diligent in his obedience to the calls of religion, the other shatteringly aware of the degraded pattern of life that held him in its grip and longing to be redeemed from it? Is it to recall us, as Lent begins, to the necessity of rule and discipline in the practice of our faith? The Pharisee can certainly remind us of that, but beware of an excessive concern with the mere externals of church life which can be to a christian as sand is said to be to an ostrich! On the one hand we need rule, on the other we are faced with an exercise in realism. We are like a group of art students setting out to make as accurate a drawing as they can of the perfectly-proportioned model set before them. In the course of the exercise their eyes will constantly be glancing up to scan the model and then down again to check the veracity of their work; not in fretful self-reproach but in a spirit of discovery. None of them will come near to the perfection of the model, but to all of them, if they have approached the project with integrity, some unsuspected meaning will have been revealed. In some way they will have grown.

It is well to remember, on this day, that the word 'Lent' derived from the old Saxon word *lencten*, meaning 'lengthening of days', and simply stands for spring, the season of new growth when the whole of nature (especially if it has emerged from a covering of snow) seems to be on the alert.

Now is the time for our hearts to be stirred, first to penitence, as we set our lives against God's perfect model in Christ; but penitence will then bring us closer to reality and to the dazzling awareness that 'Christ died for us while we were yet sinners, and that is God's own proof of his love towards us'.[1]

1. Romans 5.8 (*NEB*).

LENT 1

The campaign for the Kingdom

> Luke 4.8 '*You shall worship the Lord your God and him only shall you serve.*'

1 *Brief authority*

Battles to gain the control of government in this country are no longer fought with any hostile weapon other than the spoken or the printed word; civil wars to overthrow the British throne likewise belong to the pages of history. It is not so in some parts of today's world. When the chronicle of the twentieth century comes to be written, a frequently recurring theme will be that of the *coup d'ėtat*. Among those countries lacking a stable and long-established democracy, we have seen repeated news-reel coverage of various heads of state being deposed by heavily armed uprising. In one dramatic instance, we saw pictures of a vanquished dictator's statue being hoisted from its plinth and thrown down, leaving a gaping hole to be filled in with rubble.[1] Many of these dethroned rulers had been tyrants who, like the Caesars of ancient Rome, sought from their subjects the kind of adulation that was akin to worship. Then came a revolution and the demi-god was found - often literally - to be a dead God because he himself had worshipped the ephemeral idols of popularity and power. How often, as

1. Kwame N. Krumah of Ghana.

you've watched a new national leader sweeping to power on a flood-tide of enthusiasm, have you wondered what lay behind the fanaticism of the crowds? Was it a longing for material prosperity, a craving for novelty and excitement, or simply the fear of punitive reprisals for non-co-operation? Any one of these motives or any combination of them may be exploited in winning men's allegiance; all three of them were rejected by Jesus as ways of establishing the Kingdom of God.

In the Old Testament reading set for this Sunday under Year One in the *Alternative Service Book*, we read of a garden in which 'The Lord God made trees spring from the ground, all trees pleasant to look at and good for food'.[2] There, among the benevolent trees, lurked the adversary, waiting with all subtlety to persuade man that it is self and not God who should be worshipped. Adam was thus tempted to snatch at equality with his Maker: the battle was lost and Adam fell, ousted from the harmony of Eden.

Out beyond the last village and into the wild solitude of the desert, where he lost even the companionship of the trees, Jesus went forth to meet his adversary. There, in that arena of stones and silence, he faced the conflict within himself; the warfare of the heart waged without the support of an army, the first critical battle in the campaign for the Kingdom. In that lonely struggle it was the adversary who fell and was ousted. The reign of love as the ultimate fulfilment of his ministry had triumphed over both the rule of force and the compelling desire for popular acclaim.

2 *His battle is ours too*

'*You shall worship the Lord your God and him only shall you serve.*' This great affirmation with which the claims of the devil were finally rebuffed, was part of our Lord's heritage, the history of his people's experience in the wilderness. We must allow it to find an echo in our own heart as we go with

2. Genesis 2.90.

Christ through a world which, although it belongs historically to a wholly different era, will nevertheless confront us with the same moral choices. We may not be drawn like the power-hungry dictators to arrogate to ourselves some seat of political domination, but the temptation to manipulate others for selfish ends will still be lurking with all subtlety in the background of our everyday relationships, as will the compelling need to make an impression and to be proved always in the right. The devil will challenge us on whatever ground he finds us, tempting us to allow worldly desires to oust God's ultimate claim, enticing us to cling to idols that are really dead. In each encounter there is a potential fall either of Adam or of the adversary, each one is a personal opportunity to strengthen our discipleship.

There is a battle to be fought this Lent for every one who claims, like Bunyan's hero, the title Christian. It is part of a campaign to bring in the Kingdom of God. It is a conflict in which our weaknesses will be exposed and our cherished idols – even those we worship under the guise of religion – will be overthrown. We shall not be of much use, either to God or to others, unless we face that lonely battle, knowing that with Christ we shall 'be able to withstand in the evil day and having done all to stand'.[3]

LENT 2

A source of unity

Matthew 12.25 (*NEB*) *'No household that is divided against itself can stand.'*

1 *The scattered community*

Let us construct an imaginary scenario as if for a television documentary. The subject of this make-believe is a scattered village community which, since the building of its new

3. Ephesians 6.13.

assembly hall, has begun very tentatively to realize a corporate identity. The hall provides a point of convergence for the different sections of the population, allowing them to recognize and relate to one another in a congenial atmosphere. Tensions have consequently eased between the hard core of old villagers and the recently retired 'incomers'. There is also an improving relationship between the farming fraternity, whose place of work stands all around them, and those who travel to their jobs in the nearby town. Most of these commuters live in an enclave of 'executive' type houses at some distance from the centre of the main village.

2 *Dual carriageway divides*

Now comes the publication by the Department of Environment of its plans for a new motorway. The local section of the proposed route will not only devour many acres of good agricultural land, but it will effectively cut off the commuter belt from the rest of the village, together with a number of solitary homesteads. At first, a succession of protest meetings plus a public enquiry serve to unite the people further, but these having finally failed, the *fait accompli* of a modern dual carriageway carrying an ever increasing volume of traffic, poses its own threat to their common life. One part of the community being thereby excluded, the whole is somehow disrupted. The old divisions begin to reassert themselves.

3 *Spanning the divide*

Soon after the completion of the motorway, however, it becomes evident that further construction work is in progress, and eventually a narrow footbridge is opened spanning the roaring stream of traffic. By means of this slender structure the separated groups are given access to each other so that social contact can be restored. Like the assembly hall before it, the footbridge becomes a means of uniting the community.

All of this is a fiction, but it mirrors real life experience sufficiently well to bear out a universal axiom. We hear it on the lips of our Lord in today's passage from St Matthew; 'No household that is divided against itself can stand'. This truth is valid at every level of human existence. No village or town, no nation or group of nations, neither the world itself, nor any individual personality, can endure a divided life without losing its essential harmony.

4 *The common life in Christ*

In the Anglican Liturgy, the positive aspect of it is proclaimed when, having received the charge to 'pursue all that makes for peace and builds up our common life,'[1] the worshippers then turn to one another to offer an outward sign of peace. It is a critical moment; not only because it is expressing the bond of a common faith - if it did that and nothing more, it could become insulating rather than a reconciling agent - it is also meant to affirm an inner stability and mutual love which can extend to all manner of people and situations outside its own circle. When a church is truly able to express its common life in Christ, it is engaging in construction work; a bridge is being built; a source of unity is being developed for a divided world. Lent is a season of reappraisal and challenge, a time to set the gospel side by side with our lives and the life of our church and to see how they match up; to discover where strains are and at what points our integrity is threatened. The true test of progress along the christian way is the practical one of growth in charity; it is well expressed in the words of the General Thanksgiving which asks for such a sense of God's mercies that we may shew forth his praise not only with our lips *but in our lives by giving up ourselves to his service.*

1. *Alternative Service Book*, Rite A, p.128.

LENT 3

From Simon to Peter

Matthew 16.18 (*NEB*) '*You are Peter and on this rock I will build my Church.*'

1 *Peter: the paramount truth*

The fickleness of the weather in early spring is reflected in the restless gyration of the weathercocks upon our towers and steeples. The weathercock is a symbol of inconstancy, not merely because it turns its head to every capricious gust of wind, but because, by its shape and outline, it serves as a permanent reminder of that momentous and shameful act of inconstancy when Simon Peter denied his Lord one early morning as the cock crowed.

But what if our weather-vanes had been designed to recall, not the frailty and failure of the disciple, but the strength and reliability implied in his very name? It was Jesus himself who dubbed him, Peter, 'rock-man'. How would it be if the topmost feature of our churches were to set in relief against the sky the shape and outline of a boulder? Would that not be a more impressive symbol than the stylized image of a cockerel, especially to a generation which, in its own expressive idiom, refers to cowardice as 'chickening out'? By modern standards of managerial training, Peter's failure would exclude him once and for all as a candidate for potential leadership. What commands the recognition and respect of today's world is some sign or logo representing toughness and stability, but such a symbol cannot by itself convey the paramount truth about christian discipleship – that vocation and forgiveness are two sides of the same coin.

2 *Breakthrough and breakdown*

Simon was called and endowed with the name 'Peter', thus signifying by anticipation what he was eventually to become. Between Simon the fisherman and Peter the apostle lay a long and painful process of self-discovery. It began effectively at Caesarea Philippi when Jesus demanded of his followers a response to a question of identity, 'Who do men say I am?' Peter it was who made the true response when, in a lightning flash of insight, he saw the uniqueness of Jesus. 'You are the Christ,' he said, 'the Son of the living God.' To have discerned in the tired and travel-stained companion of their journeyings the secret of his Lordship was a striking breakthrough. But this breakthrough in understanding was straightway to be followed by a break*down*.

3 *The spider's collapse*

There is an old Danish fable which tells of a spider who descended from a high rafter by a single thread to reach the corner he had perceived to be a more congenial place to live in. Later on, when he was comfortably established, he failed to recognize the original thread on which his web depended and perfunctorily snapped it off; whereupon his whole world collapsed in ruins! There the story ends, but as far as it goes it is a parable of the beginning of Peter's discipleship, and likewise of our own. Like him, we can be overtaken by a moment of instant perception, suddenly knowing where we truly belong and seeing clearly in which direction we should go. Like him we are moved to respond - often with a burst of enthusiasm - yet something goes wrong between making the response and living it out.

4 *The way of failure and forgiveness*

Peter's moment of perception was followed by the collapse of an illusion; his false notion of messiahship had to be demolished. We hear a sinister echo of the voice of Satan in those wilderness temptations of Jesus as Peter rebuked the Lord for accepting the seemingly inglorious way of suffering and death. *And Jesus actually calls him Satan*! We do well to remember that.

But Peter's discipleship was not in ruins. Simon of Galilee would fall and fall again and need to be forgiven. Peter would eventually be established in apostleship only by the accepting and transforming grace of God. We do well also to remember this, for it can point us beyond all our inevitable failures and forgivenesses to the hope that is set before us. We shall not, in the end, be like the Danish spider, letting ourselves down to desolation, but rather using our failures to climb – like that Scottish spider once observed by Robert the Bruce – to the full and glorious potential that God can already see in us.

LENT 4

Vision and vocation

Matthew 17.2 (*NEB*) '. . . *in their presence he was transfigured . . .*'

1 *The visionary moment*

Before modern drug therapy brought it under control, the epileptic fit was regarded by many as an abnormal and frightening phenomenon. Nowadays its convulsive effects are rarely to be seen, and the moment of heightened perception which often forewarned the patient of an epileptic spasm, has been correspondingly moderated. Many of history's notable sufferers (Julius Caesar was one) have given vivid accounts of the intensity of that visionary moment preceding an attack. The prophet Mahomet, also an epileptic, is quoted – presumably in referring to the same experience – as saying that 'he visited all the dwellings of Allah, in less time than was needed to empty his pitcher of water'.[1] Dostoevsky says of one of his characters, a Russian prince, '*He remembered that during his epileptic fits, or rather*

1. Quoted by V. Gollancz in *The New Year of Grace* (Gollancz, 1960), p.390.

immediately preceding them, he had always experienced a moment or two when his whole heart, mind, and body seemed to wake up to vigour and light; when he became filled with joy and hope, all his anxieties seemed to be swept away for ever . . . "I feel then as if I understood those amazing words 'There shall be no more time' ".'

2 *Familiar scenes transformed*

Both the prophet and the prince bear witness to a fleeting experience of illumination and certainty, closely resembling the 'timeless moment' described by mystical writers of various traditions. They speak of a state of consciousness in which past, present and future are drawn together in an ineffable vision of reality. Seen thus in the light of eternity, ordinary circumstances appeared to them to be radiantly beautiful. The familiar scene, the familiar person, suddenly shone with a glory that had not been glimpsed before. They then knew, just as the three chosen disciples knew on the mount of transfiguration, that what is seen and accepted as normality in the everyday world is not an end in itself. Peter, James and John were given an ineffable glimpse of glory. It was not a glory apart from the trials and tribulations of daily life; what they were experiencing was the dazzling radiance of God's love in which ordinary circumstances, however painful, can be transformed.

3 *Half the truth*

There is an old proverb offering shrewd advice. It says, 'you may climb to the top of a mountain but you can never live there'. If only Peter on that holy mount could have comprehended this ancient truth. As it was, he grasped only half of it, and that half overwhelmed him with the sheer goodness of being with Jesus. What better than to enshrine that timeless moment? How sublime to let the pain and conflicts

2. *The Idiot* by Dostoevsky.

of the everyday world fall away, and to remain in one's self-constructed shelter, 'lost in wonder, love and praise'!

The same half-truth still prevails among some followers of Christ today, tempting them to settle for a bland unworldliness which is long on assembling together for praise, and short on involvement with a suffering society. They need to recover that sense of discovery and openness which is the true mark of God's people.

4 *We believe in the God of both mountain and valley*

The passage of scripture following on from today's gospel reveals that the dazzling vision on the mountain was an immediate prelude to the scene of a child's epileptic fit which awaited them as they returned from the heights. Jesus was involved with *both* situations. The glory of the incarnate Lord is relevant to both. The God of the mountain is the God of the valley and the disciples learn that transfiguration is united with mission. What a weight of glory lies behind those words with which we open the Creed; 'We believe in God'.

We believe in a God who shows by his life and death that glory is not separate from but *through* the struggle and the conflict.

We believe in a God who has overcome the world and can transform by his presence the ordinary circumstances of our lives so that we come to see them in a new light.

We believe in a God who became man in order that mankind, you and I – could be transfigured, and that through us the glory of his Kingdom might be realized in the world.

LENT 5

The deepest meaning

Luke 9.22 (*AV*) *'the Son of Man must suffer many things.'*

1 *Connotation of 'suffer'*

Here is a whimsical domestic picture for you mind's eye. The scene is a family living-room just after four o'clock on a winter's afternoon. A fire burns cheerfully in the grate: the family dog is comfortably established on the hearthrug. Suddenly, there is a slamming of doors signalling the return of the ten-year-old son of the house from school. He bursts into the room and throws himself down full length upon his back before the fire whereupon the dog, with unrestrained delight, jumps on to the boy's chest and starts to lick his face in welcome. The mother entering at that moment utters a sharp rebuke, 'why do you let the dog do that to you? Stop it at once!'

It is not difficult to imagine the same scene translated to an earlier century, except that one syllable in the maternal reprimand would be replaced by two, thus – 'Why do you *suffer* the dog to do that to you?' The boy is by no means suffering! Not in the currently accepted sense of the word; indeed, he is evidently enjoying the experience. Nevertheless, the older connotation of 'suffer' accurately describes the situation insofar as the boy is passive and the dog is – very much – active.

2 *Connotation of 'passion'*

Another word which has lost an earlier depth of meaning is 'passion'. In these days of banner headlines, its regular use, especially in popular journalism, is generally in a sensational context involving either sex or violence. It has therefore come to stand for something active and extreme. But if we could return to the creative culture that produced such inspired musical works as the *St Matthew Passion*, we might recover an older and more profound idea.

3 *The suffering love of the Lord*

The common derivation of 'passive' and 'passion'[1] points us to the theme of this second Sunday before Good Friday which, from time immemorial, has been given the name 'Passion Sunday' because, on that day, Jesus began to make open predictions of his coming ordeal. Clearly, in the most common usage of the word he did indeed 'suffer' extreme pain and torment, but behind it all was another meaning; the one that inspired our Victorian forebears to take the text they loved so well and work it into embroidered samplers to hang in their living rooms: '*SUFFER THE LITTLE CHILDREN TO COME UNTO ME*'.[2] It reminded them of the time when Jesus overruled the disciples who were trying to distance the children from him.

4 *Finding his meaning*

Jesus suffered the children to come; just as in the last days of his incarnate life he suffered the crowds with loud hosannas and waving palms to hail him as Saviour-King and, less than a week later, suffered himself to be bound, scourged and mocked. In each circumstance part of the meaning of 'Passion' is revealed. At the centre of it all we behold a figure of enormous dignity and freedom. He had no freedom in the currently accepted sense of the word and, yet, in the deeper context of selfless love he was completely and utterly free.

This Sunday commemorates the beginning of the most significant fortnight in the world's history. It brings to a climax the revelation of God in Christ, showing us a God who is prepared to enter into, to accept and turn to glory, all

1. *Pascho* (Greek), To suffer, endure, experience.

2. Mark 10.14.

that man does to him. Our natural reaction is to rebuke him as Simon Peter once did, 'Why do you let them do that to you?' The deepest part of us longs to reach out to him and discover *his* meaning in the things that are happening to us, especially as we encounter hardship, pain and adversity. If, in some tiny way, as we cope with each circumstance, we reflect his attitude both to the children coming to him and to the conflict, then we are sharing in his passion. We are no longer inhabiting a narrow circumscribed world; we are entering into *his* world. Here there is suffering, yes, but there is peace and joy and true freedom.

PALM SUNDAY

Prelude to Calvary

Matthew 21.10 (*NEB*) '*When he entered Jerusalem the whole city went wild with excitement.*'

1 *Effervescent enthusiasm is short-lived*

Scenes of wild and hysterical jubilation would have been looked upon by a former generation as out of keeping with the natural reserve of the British. Nowadays such outbursts are common place. Emotional fervour of the kind whipped up by American-style cheer leaders has become a feature of popular sport and entertainment in this country, affecting both spectators and performers. The spectacle of English cricketers embracing one another at the fall of an opponent's wicket, is far removed from the sober and dignified image of the game as it was once viewed from the members' pavilion at Lords.

One characteristic of these effervescent feelings is that they are short-lived. Think of the excitement of children at the end of term. Their high expectations and even higher spirits are liable so soon to dissolve into boredom and inactivity, causing parents secretly to long for their return to school. And not without reason! The demands of the time-table may present a chastening contrast to the easy-going freedom of the holidays, but it is within the regular routine that discoveries are made and horizons are widened.

2 *Rapture and riot*

A more disturbing aspect of collective emotional excitement is its tendency to escalate into violence. Pageants and processions setting out in a spirit of Mardi Gras with accompanying policemen who are themselves in friendly and festive mood, may encounter units of the same force equipped with riot-gear before the proceedings are over. Rapture and riot, as we have learned from the bitter experience of several British soccer clubs, are two sides of a communal coin; there seems to be no shortage of trouble-makers waiting to incite a change of mood from one to the other. How readily can delirious supporters worshipping their current idols be transformed into a mob bent upon destruction.

3 *Acclaiming a hero*

The blindness and fickleness of popular enthusiasm is no modern phenomenon. We shall see it reflected in a change of attitude towards our Lord as we follow events in Jerusalem during the last week of his earthly life. The narrative begins today on a note of wild excitement, with Jesus at the centre of a street demonstration, being acclaimed by the crowd as a folk hero. The atmosphere – against the background of the forthcoming Passover festival – was one of celebration, yet it contained an element of nationalist aggression. If the setting were transposed to our own time, there would be banners bearing slogans and the brick walls along the route would echo their message in crude letters, sprayed on with aerosol paint: 'JESUS OF NAZARETH RULES OK' 'ROMANS OUT'. Expectations were running high, enthusiasm for a King-Messiah were at fever pitch. Jesus was willing, for the time, to offer himself to their hosannas, thus fulfilling the prophecy of Zechariah,[1] although he was aware that their ecstatic welcome was based upon a distorted and illusory hope and would be short-lived. Soon the crowds, incited by the trouble-makers planted among them by his enemies, would be bent upon his destruction. Their initial rejoicing at the arrival of a liberator belied the true means of liberation. It was to come through the cross.

4 *Beyond emotion*

Palm Sunday is not a joyous celebration; it is a prelude to Calvary. The main gospel for today speaks not of the triumphal entry but of the Passion. The Liturgy is pointing us beyond an emotional response and towards a deeper encounter with Christ in which horizons are widened and new – often painful – truths are discovered. In the events of Holy Week we see God in action in the face both of popular acclaim and of utter rejection. Palm Sunday was a fair weather gathering; on Good Friday the storm clouds darkened the sky. Our Lord shows us by his response how each experience is transformed by love.

Let us, as far as we can, stay with him in the events of this week. Let us identify his crisis with our lesser crises and make some positive remembrance of his pain and humiliation, so that, when we come next Sunday to proclaim his victory over sin and death, our rejoicing will be the greater because we have shared in his Passion.

1. Zechariah 9.9.

EASTER DAY

The loving stranger

John 20.14 (*RSV*) *'She did not know it was Jesus.'*

1 *The Button Boy*

The many old sailors who mourn the passing of the famous training ship HMS *Ganges* will remember with lively affection the role of the Button Boy.

He was the young sailor cadet chosen from among his contemporaries to stand on the tiny platform at the very summit of the seventy-five-foot mast which was manned lower down for the end-of-term display by the rest of the class. Not everyone had the nerve or the agility or the balance to do it, but there were always some among those not chosen who still reckoned that, given the chance, they would have made a good Button Boy.

Among them, in one particular year, was a certain cheeky character who took on a 'dare' from his messmates and, when the parade ground was deserted, climbed the mast and stood to attention in solitary splendour on the button: an exploit strictly against the rules of the establishment.

Sure enough, as he half expected and feared, he was duly summoned to appear before the Captain - a formidable figure to a young cadet in those far-off days - and sure enough, as he fully expected and feared, he received a monumental rebuke. The skipper stopped his leave and condemned him to every kind of dirty and degrading extra duty; in fact, just as he had expected and feared.

What he could never have predicted was the change which then transformed his Captain. The boy suddenly found himself confronted by a total stranger. There were the four rings on the sleeve and the gold braid on the cap, but the face underneath the cap now wore a smile, and the hand in the sleeve had reached into the pocket and fetched out a ten-shilling note (a significant sum in those days). 'Here,' said the Captain, patting him paternally on the head, 'that's for your courage. Now get out of here and don't come before me again.'

That boy left the Captain's office with a threefold image. First, the towering reprimand which he had thought he deserved; then the confrontation with a total stranger who made him feel in some secure way accepted, even loved; and finally the brisk ejection into the daily routine, but now with a changed outlook: a telling experience before the dangerous adventure of wartime seagoing.

2 *The sea is his*

Once at sea, having launched out from *terra firma*, especially in a smallish ship, there is a curious sense of being committed to an unpredictable element. It can give rise to sudden destructive storms, but it can also give a sense of leading one on to wider and exciting horizons.

'The sea is his and he made it', says the jewish psalmist, but he says it with an air of pained surprise, perhaps remembering the sudden squalls that could blow up on the inland sea; certainly recalling Genesis 1 and the chaos and darkness that was upon the face of the deep.

The sea is his and he made it! That unruly, destructive, yet also strangely creative element. Do you not remember how they threw Jonah overboard to try and calm it down? And how Jesus stood up in the boat and quelled it by a word?

3 *Who is this stranger?*

Jesus' disciples were astonished and afraid: not of the storm at sea any more, but of this stranger who, having been cosily asleep in the boat, could make the elements secure by his word. They were scared, and he rebuked them for being scared. It was a towering rebuke: 'Why are you such cowards? Where is your faith?' And they said to one another, 'Who can this be?' Who is this stranger who draws us from the familiar to the creatively strange, who makes us feel secure and yet rebukes us? For he *was* a stranger, even to those who were close to him and placed their hopes in him, and even they repeatedly failed to recognize him.

There was the Easter stranger in the garden (Mary Magdalene mistook him for the gardener); and the Easter stranger on the shore; and the Easter stranger on the road to Emmaus, who walked beside the two disciples and rebuked them for not grasping the connection between suffering and glory.

4 *The call of the stranger*

This Eastertide Jesus calls us, as he called them, to something genuinely new and alive. But he rebukes us. He rebukes us for the challenges we refuse to accept, for the barriers that erect to preserve our security, for our nostalgia for what we call the 'good old days'. He rebukes us because he is alive and wants to confront us again as the stranger calling us forward to something new, even painful.

When our religion becomes the servant of nostalgia, when the Church becomes so set in her ways that she cannot hear the call of Jesus the stranger to new visions, then she becomes monumentally irrelevant, and what she does in her synods and committees is little more than self-justification.

We are not meant to be a memorial society commemorating the past deeds and words of Jesus, but a community in which he lives and acts. A community prepared to be renewed again and again.

Like that cheeky, misguided, self-styled Button Boy, we know we are not innocent and Jesus will never pretend that we are. What he will do, by sending us briskly out into the world, is to proclaim that we are accepted, forgiven and loved beyond the worst that we can do.

Inexhaustible hope

Mark 16.6 (*AV*) *'He has risen; he is not here.'*

Christian Aid week might be known in the hearts of some of our brave door-to-door volunteers as 'Nightmare Dread week!' They tremble, having dropped gift envelopes through people's letterboxes, at the prospect of returning to knock at the same doors to collect them. Nine times out of ten there is no reason whatever to be apprehensive. Even where people are not generous, they are grudgingly cooperative. It's the odd case of the refusal, the rebuff, and most especially the door slammed in the face, that gives rise to their dread.

A shut door is such a formidable symbol of rejection. One's heart goes out to some of the deputations who foregather outside Number 10 on those occasions when the door is opened momentarily to receive their petition and then is firmly closed again.

1 *A happy ending?*

It could be said that the life story of Jesus of Nazareth begins and ends with that same symbol of rejection. The door of the inn shut against his pregnant mother and, finally, the great stone door blocking the entrance to his tomb.

Did not both these incidents, however, have a happy ending, and is that not why we come to church at Christmas and have now come at Easter? To celebrate a happy ending? . . . but such a cosy view obscures a deeper truth.

The ending we do well to remember is the one that the world of power structures and vested interests and the sheer determination of people not to have their lives interfered with, tried to make when they slammed the doors on Christ. That world still exists and is still hostile to him and to what he stands for. What Easter does is to set in motion a process to defeat it. What Easter also does is to draw us to one side or the other in that process.

So we do not come primarily to celebrate a happy ending but – if we are genuinely seeking to offer ourselves for the healing of this world – to accept our part of the freedom that Jesus brings. Freedom to say 'no' to a world of violence and threat that sees force as the only means to its end. This freedom could only come through the rejection of the cross and the exclusion of the tomb.

It was at the tomb that the women (coming as so many do today to tend the place where the memory is) heard those four short unforgettable words 'He is not here'.

2 *One door shuts; another opens*

The gospel then tells us that they said nothing to anybody for they were afraid. How familiar to all of us (not only the Christian Aid volunteers) is that state of bewildered apprehension. When we are in a situation that radically disrupts our plans and expectations it makes us afraid. It puts to death our misguided assumptions and illusions. When the door is slammed on our personal hopes we die a little death.

Beethoven once said 'It's a poor sort of man that doesn't know how to die. I have known how to die since I was in my teens.' He was not, I believe, talking about clinical death.

Every acceptance of a new and challenging call to commitment helps in our renewal; every death to the fantasies and illusions that have been sustaining our ego. One door slams and the Lord moves to throw open another. Therein is the inexhaustible hope of Easter. He has risen; he is not here.

EASTER 1

Bread – the giver is the gift

John 6.32 (*JB*) '*I am the bread of life.*'

1 *The 'fight for food'*

The reproduction of old posters is a growth industry. Styles and designs originally developed for public communication are discovered, two or three generations later, to have acquired widespread popular appeal as decorative art. One such poster produced during the time of acute shortages in the late 1940s was first intended for display in canteens and restaurants as propaganda in the so called 'fight for food'. The campaign symbol was a broadsword held aloft to reveal a stylized ear of wheat superimposed on the blade.[1] The caption alongside it read, 'DON'T ASK FOR BREAD UNLESS YOU REALLY NEED IT'. What an apt introduction to the theme for this Sunday, '*The Bread of Life*'.

2 *Enough for gratitude not greed*

When food is rationed, the procuring of supplies becomes a precarious day-to-day affair. This is a familiar experience for many deprived communities today, just as it was for post-war Britons and post-exodus Israelites during their flight across the desert. There could be no opportunity for the hysterical stockpiling which often marks our more affluent consumer societies. The patient British housewife queueing for her meagre loaf reminds us of the ancient Jew waiting each morning to gather his day's supply of perishable manna. Enough for gratitude but never enough for greed. Like the vanished era of scarcity evoked by the old posters, the experience of being fed in the wilderness of Sinai became for the jewish nation a vivid folk memory. It

1. A picture of the poster in its original setting can be seen in *Memory Lane*, a photographic album published by J.M. Dent & Sons Ltd., 1980.

was recalled, according to John's gospel, by another generation in another wilderness after an alfresco meal of bread and fish.

3 *A successor to Moses?*

When our Lord fed five thousand hungry Galileans, there were some for whom he seemed to be tapping the very wellsprings of their national history. Their ancestors under Moses' leadership, had, they knew, received sustenance when they were fainting in the desert. The food then, had appeared to come from above, from the Jewish heaven of sky and clouds. This man, by a strange and mighty act out there in the wild, had likewise satisfied the people's hunger, but *he had interposed himself between heaven and earth.* He had taken ordinary bread in his own hands and blessed it! Their impressions were confused and they came to him in their perplexity seeking a sign of his authority. They were looking for some gift - like the manna - direct from above, to connect heaven with earth and to confirm Jesus as the natural successor to Moses; one who would bring God nearer to them and provide for their material needs. They wanted a leader and they wanted bread.

4 *The doctor is the medicine*

In the obituary of a well-beloved country doctor who had remained in the same practice for fifty years, it was said of him that 'the doctor was the medicine'.[2] The physician and the physic had, in some profound way, become integrated, so that a visit from him was a healing event, whether or not it issued in prescriptions or treatment. New patients might crave for pills and potions, old patients knew that however necessary these might be, they were secondary to the person who prescribed them. This experience, at the natural level of the relationship between doctor and patient, is like a

2. His gravestone in Pleshey churchyard in Essex bears the simple inscription 'Hugh Douglas Robertson. Physician. 1906–1983.'

fingerpost pointing in the direction of eternal truth. The jews craved for natural food, our Lord answered them with a supernatural disclosure, 'I am the Bread of Life'. He himself is the gift he brings; the link between heaven and earth for which they yearned is a person. The doctor is indeed the medicine, not just for Israel, but for all mankind and for eternity.

At every Eucharist the natural and supernatural significance of bread becomes integrated. Our Lord renews his offer of nourishment, sustenance and strength for our spiritual life as we consume his gift of himself into our natural bodies. The bread of life is eternally available; it cannot be purchased or hoarded up but has to be received afresh at each opportunity like the manna in the wilderness. He is ready to give according to our hunger. Let us pray that we shall never be separated from him by lack of appetite.

EASTER 2

God knows and cares

John 10.11 '*I am the good shepherd.*'

1 *Situations vacant*

A typical advertisement in the classified columns of a current newspaper might read as follows:

> Lively and energetic priest/minister required for active and responsive congregation. Large and well-appointed church, serving a developing community, offers busy and varied sphere of work. An exciting challenge for the right person.

Exciting indeed *for the right person*! The image presented by such announcements, however, suggests that for the wrong person the post would carry a grave risk of exhaustion and eventual collapse. The need to be still and to listen, waiting regularly upon God in quiet and prayerful attention to his will, is rarely made explicit in ministerial job-descriptions. The Church must beware of appointing its pastors by the sole criterion of success in external activities. They need to be free to say 'no' to a round of incessant demands that will drain away their spiritual resources. Free with the quality of freedom that we see in Jesus.

Consider some of the hypothetical job vacancies for which Jesus would have been eligible to apply:

> Director of counselling service required, with experience of personal, in-depth interviewing. Able to take responsibility for the training of a team of assistants.
>
> Expert communicator needed to work either with small groups or large public meetings. Experience of outdoor public-speaking essential.
>
> Skilled carpenter wanted. Ideal candidate will have gained varied experience within small family business.

2 *Two insights into God*

Our Lord might properly have filled any one of these vacancies, and having given his life to it been able, with truth, to claim that he was a good counsellor/communicator/carpenter.

In fact, what he did with his life was to make of it a gift. To give it away absolutely in love and compassion, so that we receive his 'I am' sayings at a deeper level; for example, 'I am the way, the truth and the life', 'I am the resurrection and I am life', or 'I am the good shepherd'. This last example occurs in the gospel for today, when Jesus singles out two particular qualities of the good shepherd: 'I know my own sheep and my sheep know me . . . and I lay down my life for the sheep'. Close and personal knowledge of each member of the flock, and willingness to put his life on the line in their defence. Knowing them and offering his life for them. Two profound insights into the nature of God as we see it revealed in Jesus.

3 *Knowing*

There is a cartoon in the *Peanuts* series[1] in which the dog Snoopy is lying forlornly on top of his kennel in the rain, until Charlie Brown comes along and shouts at him, 'Get inside, you stupid dog!' Snoopy brightens up at once and comes down, thinking 'Somebody cares!'

If we can embrace the idea of God as the good shepherd, we shall be brought like Snoopy into the realization that we are known and cared for personally. It is as if God calls us by name, saying, 'John/Mary, it is good to be with you'. We come then to realize that our God is not remote and awe-inspiring, but as intimate and homely as a boy calling his dog in from the rain. The world is looking for triumphalism, for superstars and world-beaters; but how can you enter into an authentic relationship with a superstar? Like Mary Magdalene in the Easter garden, we need to be identified by name to know that we are loved and affirmed. That is not in any sense to deny God's transcendence and distinctness from us, but rather to safeguard its true meaning. We can still proclaim that Jesus is Lord, but let us understand from the second characteristic of the shepherd mentioned in the gospel, what kind of Lord.

4 *Risking*

Peaceful English vistas of sheep, grazing beneath boughs of apple blossom can easily lead us to sentimentalize the conception of the Lord as shepherd. 'The Church is always tempted,' wrote Eric Abbott, 'to prophesy smooth things rather than hard things.'[2] In fact, the true shepherd, like the

1. Charles M. Schultz, (Coronet).

2. Eric Abbott, *The Compassion of God and the Passion of Christ: a Scriptural Meditation for Lent* (Bles, 1963), p.46.

true pastor, is exposed to extremes of hardship and to the possibility of tragedy. Jesus unhesitatingly accepted the rigours of a tough, itinerant life, with the inevitable risk of rejection and suffering. In that total commitment leading to the cross we see the truth of God's sacrificial love. It is to that picture of Lordship that christians are called to be faithful. A busy, success-oriented Church will find it difficult to hear the call of the Lord the shepherd, which is to be still and know that he, in all his loving vulnerability, is God.

EASTER 4

Day by day to God

John 14.6 (*NEB*) '*I am the way*'

1 *The travelling diarist*

A personal diary is a thing to be treasured. Not a mere list of engagements but an individual record of events and experiences which, as any committed diarist will tell you, more than repays the discipline of writing it up. There is an evident connection between the French word *jour* meaning 'day' and the word 'journal'; together they may be linked with the word 'journey', bringing to mind a picture of the diarist as a traveller. At the end of each day we may imagine him having pitched his tent, sitting down to retrace in his mind the distance travelled on the last stretch of the journey. He recalls the landmarks, the encounters and conversations, endeavouring to capture the 'feel' of the day and to record the highlights in his journal. For christians living in an activist culture, bombarded on all sides by noisy distraction, the image is a valuable one. How essential to our identity as followers of Christ that we give time to ponder each day's happenings, seeking his meaning in them and savouring them as part of our own pilgrimage.

From the earliest times the symbol of the journey has been used by chroniclers of the christian life, issuing naturally, as it does from our Lord's own life and teaching. His reference to himself in today's gospel as 'the way' reflects the same symbol; it was a title that must have specially appealed to the early Church, for in the Acts of the Apostles we find both its members and their enemies using it as a term for the new religion.[1]

For us who are on the same journey of faith, the symbol remains deeply significant. It speaks to us of detachment, direction and destination.

2 *Detachment*

The barnacle, according to marine biologists, is a curious example of evolution in reverse. There was a time when it swam freely around in the ocean, now it simply settles upon some solid base like the hull of a ship and adheres to it so tightly that it cannot easily be dislodged. The institutional Church is always at risk from the barnacle syndrome, however well-appointed its buildings, however illustrious its worship. It cannot ultimately be true to the gospel unless its members are ready to hold nothing permanent other than the loving will of God and are open to be guided day by day into all such good works as he has prepared for them to walk in.

3 *Direction*

Subtle monitoring systems using infra-red cameras enable us nowadays to observe at close range the nocturnal habits of woodland creatures. We are able to see the fox, the badger and the hedgehog going about their affairs and seeming to follow a well defined track; occasionally stopping to take stock of their position and then pressing on as if drawn by some invisible homing device. Christians likewise who are following 'the way' are not wandering by chance. We have

1. Acts 19.9.

come from God, we belong to God and are destined for God.[2] The distant prospect is not always visible nor does it need to be if, day by day there is a taking stock, seeking the direction in which the Lord is leading. In order to do this there needs to be before nightfall a slowing down, when, like the travel-stained wayfarer, we metaphorically pitch our tent and relax into God's presence. There, as we gently run a mental video of the day's events, we ask him to show us what he wants us to see in our response to the things that have happened and where he wants us to go on the morrow. It is a moment for penitence, thanksgiving and hope.

4 *Destination*

'*We will lay us down in peace and take our rest*', '*For it is thou, Lord, only that makest us dwell in safety*'. The ancient monastic office of Compline, from which this versicle and response are taken, belongs, like the habit of keeping a journal, to the tranquil moments at the end of the day. It moves us from the realm of thinking into the realm of trusting, reminding us that the christian journey finds its ultimate fulfilment in God's eternal changelessness. The disciplines of journalling and prayer thus link together the dimensions of time and eternity and disclose the promise of heaven that is contained in both. Our Lord in the gospel speaks of 'dwelling places', a word that can refer either to temporary or to permanent habitations; to the stepping stones across the water or to the final security of the river bank which they help the traveller to attain.

We are not committed to some vague longing for an afterlife that somehow survives death. The attainment of heaven does not entail dying but turning ever more openly and fully to God, receiving glimpses of his glory along the way. We know that he is drawing us on through the ordinary joys and sufferings of our journey and our journalling, into the glory and mystery of his love.

2. A theme underlying the *Spiritual Exercises* of St Ignatius of Loyola.

EASTER 5

The light of the Spirit's leading

John 16.13 (*RSV*) '*When the Spirit of Truth comes, he will guide you into all the truth.*'

1 *Popular performers*

With the closing down of the Edwardian music hall and Vaudeville theatres, the art of the illusionist might have been expected to pass into obscurity along with many of the old-time variety acts. Magicians and conjurors, however, despite the changing face of popular entertainment, are still in regular demand, as they have been at various periods throughout history. The best of them are to be seen at peak viewing times performing under the glare of studio lighting and the uncompromising scrutiny of the television cameras. There will nevertheless be certain viewers who, when an illusionist of any kind appears on the screen, promptly switch off the set, because their reaction to the art of the magician is negative or even hostile. These are of a type which has no time for superstition or credulity; in any situation their dominant impulse is to get at the facts and to analyse them objectively. They are therefore unwilling to be taken in by the illusionist, even within the context of relaxation or entertainment. They know that at the heart of his presentation there must be a deception; what is apparently happening has no counterpart in reality. What is being done is not the truth.

2 *A living reality*

Among the variety artists of the old-time music hall were the cross-talk comedians whose routines of song and patter might have included such 'chestnuts' as this . . .

Father to Son 'I want an explanation and I want the truth'.

Son to Father 'Make up your mind, Dad, you can't have both.'

This is unsophisticated humour, long out of fashion, but it serves to remind us that truth is more than what we are asking for when we bid an erring child to tell us the truth and not to tell a lie. St John in his gospel presents truth as a living reality probing like a powerful searchlight into the darkness and duplicity of evil. Truth, according to John, is not merely to be spoken or thought of or believed, it is something to be *done*. It goes beyond the intellectual concepts of factual analysis and into the realm of experience.

3 *Disclosure by degrees*

The function of the Holy Spirit is to lead us into that experience of active truth, not by a single overwhelming revelation, but step by step as we are able to receive it. A modern stained glass window by John Piper in the chapel of the Robinson College at Cambridge presents the visitor with a visual parable. It is an abstract composition in which dark and sombre colours gradually merge into a climactic golden sunburst. The chapel is so designed that the window cannot be seen in its entirety from any one position. Its full beauty is disclosed in stages as one progresses around the building. Like the chapel visitor, the christian has to move on through changing perspectives of truth, open to the leading of the Spirit, growing always into greater meaning and finding at every stage a deeper awareness of God. *Unlike* the chapel visitor, the christian's discoveries are not limited by the frame of a window: 'Onto the unending end of endless eternity new astonishments will keep breaking in on us in Jesus Christ'.[1] The inexhaustible truth into which the Spirit leads is not a set of lofty ideals which have no counterpart in reality. It does not depreciate our dignity and intelligence with subtle half-truths like some of the modern illusionists, not only in show business but in advertising and politics. It is God's ultimate reality shown forth in action which is Christ himself, by whom, with whom and in whom we offer our worship and our lives.

1. A.J. Gossip, *Interpreter's Bible*, Vol. 8, p.732.

THE SUNDAY AFTER ASCENSION DAY

Two different worlds

Luke 24.52 (*NEB*) '*They worshipped him and then went back to Jerusalem full of joy.*'

1 *Fighting for an ideal world*

The cross-channel ferry was approaching Dieppe on a fine calm day in early June. Two groups of travellers had assembled on the upper deck to catch the first glimpse of their common destination, Normandy. They were bound nevertheless for two different worlds.

One party was planning to visit Normany's great centres of civilization where treasures of art and architecture speak of a long-established and glorious culture. The others were on a commemorative journey around the battle-fields of the Second World War where rows of well-tended graves bear witness to the horror and tragedy of human conflict. Two different worlds! The heaven of humanity's highest aspirations and the blood-stained hell of war.

We might have hoped that those who fought and died with such tenacity and courage on the tragic plains of Normandy had enabled the spirit of man to expand again; to recover a high ideal of civilization. They were fighting, it was said, to make the world a better place; so that life could be fuller, richer, more gracious. D-day on the Normandy beaches happened nearly half a century ago. When we look for the marks of civilization now, it seems that in almost five decades we have not achieved heaven in exchange for hell. All the longings expressed in the wartime songs and slogans have not been realized. No doubt the material benefits are potentially greater, but we are far from achieving that ideal society of which men have always dreamed and which many believed would come once the evil of Nazism had been vanquished.

Jesus did not think that way at all, according to the distinguished methodist writer, Neville Ward. He says,

> It is not possible to find in his words any hint that he looked forward to the gradual elimination of evil in a universal peace and order that some future generation would enjoy. No kind of this worldly futurism would have made any sense to him. His mind was occupied with the ultimate and with now, with heaven and earth.[1]

The gospels accordingly represent Jesus as belonging to two worlds. They depict the world of a man with no proper home of his own, travelling the dusty roads of Palestine with his disciples, often tired to the point of exhaustion, achieving none of the material success that people generally desire for themselves. At the same time, they reveal the world of a man who walked so closely with God, that in each of his encounters we can see God's sovereignty shining through him.

This festival season of Ascensiontide breaks down the barrier between the two worlds. It proclaims gloriously that our God reigns, while at the same time affirming that in Christ he has worn the bloodstained garments of the crucified victim amid the conflicts and cruelties of our world. The disciples who walked with him and were devastated by his death, returned home rejoicing after their farewell blessing from the risen Jesus. Hardly a normal reaction in earthly terms! We do not usually rejoice when we are finally parted from someone we love, but they had penetrated the barrier between earth and heaven. The assurance of his word was echoing in their hearts, 'Know that I am with you always; yes, to the end of time.'[2]

In his abiding presence they would be able to walk in both worlds.

1. From *Beyond Tomorrow* by J. Neville Ward, (Epworth Press, 1981), p.31.
2. Matthew 28.20 (*JB*).

3 *Bringing heaven to earth*

'The fundamental reason why this world looks so distorted and hopeless is that we no longer really believe that a more important world exists or that this world only makes sense in the light of that unseen permanent order.' These words were part of a broadcast from St Martins in the Fields in early June 1946[3] on the eve of the post-war victory parade. More than forty years later they retain their central truth that our western society is largely bounded by the standards of only one world, the world of material achievement. In Ascensiontide terms, achievement means recognizing the sovereign lordship of Christ over all our lives and affairs. It means looking outwards to that unseen permanent world to which the great spires and monuments of Normandy bear witness, and allowing it to shine through all our encounters.

The simple elements that we use for Communion, the bread and the wine, they too belong to both worlds. They are part of the ordinary basic nourishment of life but in Jesus' hands they are the means of bringing heaven to earth.

PENTECOST

Borne up by the Spirit

> Deuteronomy 32.11 (*AV*) '*As an eagle . . . beareth them on her wings.*'

I watched the ungainly attempts of some large, web-footed bird to gather speed along the ground for take off. It flapped and waddled along at a shambling trot until, suddenly, it was airborne. Rising into its new dimension it became a thing of grace and beauty. Not every run-up had been successful; several times it had come to grief, overcome by its own weight.

3. From *A Great View* by Eric S. Loveday, (Skeffington, 1951), p.187.

1 *Lost for words*

I was reminded of my own leaden-footed efforts to put profound experience into language; written or spoken: so seldom does it take wing; the right words just do not come, and this is not an uncommon experience to judge by many a televized interview.

> 'How did you feel when you heard that your son was safe?'
> 'Fantastic!'
> 'What was it like to score the winning goal?'
> 'Magic!'
> 'Can you describe the moment when you shook hands with the Princess?'
> 'Great!'

The people being interviewed found it impossible to put their unique experience into words, to reveal outwardly what had affected them so deeply within.

Their problem is shared by the author of the Acts of the Apostles who, in attempting to describe the event we commemorate today, had to stretch language to breaking point. In the end, as the author struggled to illustrate the unique phenomenon that had transformed the lives of one small group of disciples, he remembered the Old Testament imagery surrounding the presence of God and likened it, as the prophets had done, to nature's most powerful agents, wind and fire. This was the closest he could come to describing that power which brought such a profound inward experience.

Of the three great festivals, Christmas, Easter and Witsun, the third is the one to attract the least popular support in many churches. Is this partly because of the difficulty of conveying its meaning in words? The birth of a baby is straightforward enough, so is the discovery of an empty tomb; but what of this hidden, dynamic changing of cowards into heroes? This is not so easy to put down in black and white.

2 *A church taking off*

There was, however, no problem over reporting the subsequent results of what happened at Pentecost. The rest of the book of Acts is devoted to it, and what exciting reading it makes! It is about a church taking off into a new dimension. There has been a transformation. Another image comes to mind, out of personal experience, recalling a visit to the local reference library. It was deserted except for one other reader seated on a small upright wooden chair. The book he held had come from the very topmost shelf, and I wondered how he had managed to reach it. All was made clear when he came to replace the volume. He simply stood up and, grasping the back of the chair which was hinged, folded it outwards, thus turning the whole contraption into a short flight of steps. That which had supported his seated weight now became his means of ascent. The same structure, but changed in form and function; transformed.

A true celebration of Pentecost must open today's church to the possibility of being changed in unexpected ways. We recall the attitude of expectancy among those first disciples as they gathered together to await the promised gift. Poised to take off in whatever direction the Spirit led, yet knowing that the same Spirit would bear them up. There is a deep and urgent need for us, who are overcome by the weight of conventional 'Churchianity', to recover the sure and steady conviction that the Holy Spirit of God can transform our particular situation; not necessarily with the force of a gale or the heat of a furnace. His presence may be felt as a firm but gentle nudge in a certain direction, enabling us to do that thing which hitherto we have been afraid to do, to opt in rather than to opt out. Not just to sit there but to start ascending into a new dimension.

3 *Stirred up*

A strikingly vivid illustration of the way God deals with his people comes to us in Deuteronomy chapter 32, verse 11

(*AV*): 'As an eagle stirreth up her nest, fluttereth over her young, spreadeth abroad her wings, taketh them, beareth them on her wings'.

When the time comes for the eaglets to fly, the mother bird disturbs the cosiness of the nest in order to motivate the young for the great adventure. They are to entrust themselves to the upholding power of the air, yet, even as they take off, she will hover over them ready to swoop down to the rescue of those who might come to grief.

May this great feast of Pentecost see a threefold increase in the Church:

1. In the urgency of our expectation that the Spirit will come.
2. In our readiness to undertake new ventures by his leading.
3. In our dependence upon him in all that we do undertake.

TRINITY SUNDAY

Trinity experienced

John 14.17 (*JB*) '. . . *You know him, because he is with you he is in you.*'

1 *Storm force*

If you were told about one whose face had been gashed right across, causing the loss of an eye, you might at first assume it to be the result either of an accident or of some vicious assault. Understandably so. You might then be relieved to hear that neither the victim nor the agent of the injury were animate beings. The damaged face in this instance belonged to a stained glass figure; part of the west window of an Essex church which had taken the full force of a freak storm on

Whitsun Day 1985. Hailstones the size of golf balls had destroyed every pane of unprotected glass in the area; car windscreens were shattered and not a single greenhouse remained standing. This was a capricious tempest, sweeping along on a random path, bringing destruction in its wake yet leaving untouched the property of certain awestruck bystanders who were near enough to watch it pass by. Nature, when it releases dynamic force, can still leave men feeling puny and helpless.

2 *Pagan gods and mindless violence*

In ancient times such phenomena would have been attributed to the whim of a pagan deity, for the gods of old were believed to be cruel and capricious, using the earth and its mortals as their playthings. Social violence, of a kind with which we are all too familiar in our own day, would similarly have been seen as the sport of those pagan gods whose amoral character fell far below the highest human qualities. Indeed, in these turbulent times, it might seem as if the old gods have returned to torment the earth.

Modern man, however, is no longer able to ascribe the ills of his world to ancient deities. The word most often on the lips of those reporting some act of vandalism or violence is 'mindless'. In that context it has a number of synonyms; 'pointless', 'purposeless', 'meaningless'. No longer can we lay the blame for some destructive outbreak upon the gods. Arguments and accusations may reverberate around its possible cause, but there is a widespread sense of the ultimate meaninglessness of it all. Modern man, on the evidence of what he sees on his television screen, is inclined to endorse the verdict of Shakespeare's Macbeth, that life is . . . 'a tale told by an idiot full of sound and fury signifying nothing'.

3 *All shall be well*

Christians, who find themselves equally shocked and confused by the world of today, have to face up to the suggestion that belief in a personal God is wishful thinking. In the face of inexplicable disasters, the God we worship, say the cynics, is an illusion; no more than a childish fantasy. Can I bring myself to believe that? Is is true that chaos and anarchy have the final word?

Let us take a simple domestic picture. A toddler wakes up in the night crying in the dark and his mother hastens to comfort and reassure him. Listen to what she says 'There, there, hush, don't cry, it will be all right.' The cynics might declare this to be a monstrous deception. How can she affirm that it will be all right in a world containing terrorism, cancer and the threat of nuclear destruction? Yet our deepest instincts endorse her action and we seem to hear echoing down the centuries the voice of Mother Julian of Norwich, after horrendous suffering, proclaiming that 'All shall be well and all shall be well and all manner of things shall be well'. The worst holocaust seems unable to quench the deep-seated hope that is within man.

4 *Trinity is experienced*

The festival we celebrate today affirms that our hope is not illusonry. It seeks to enrich the way we believe, bringing meaning to the name and nature of the true God by calling him Trinity; three persons and one God. The Trinity is not just a theory, it interprets the undoubted facts of the Bible and of christian experience in relation to God.

In the Old Testament he is experienced as the God of all the families of Israel, sometimes stern, sometimes demanding, but known with certainty to be compassionate, merciful and faithful. In the New Testament he becomes incarnate to stand before men so that when they look at Jesus, they know what life is for.

He is not, then, experienced fully until he comes, as he

has to generations of christians, to be the go-between-God, the Holy Spirit making men aware of his presence within, transforming living into life.

'The Trinity cannot be explored except from the centre. And what is the centre? It is the Love of God.' These are the words of the late Austin Farrer in his book *Lord I believe.*[1] They point us to the supreme truth that, in contrast to the pagan gods, our God matches and surpasses the highest human quality, because he is a Trinity of love. The final word is not with tragedy but love, yet it is love shown *through* tragedy, because at the centre of our faith is a cross. Until we range ourselves alongside a suffering God whose pain is the pain of the storm victim, the cancer victim and the victim of the holocaust, we cannot begin to offer to a troubled world the hope and reassurance it so desperately needs.

PENTECOST 2

Readiness for life

I Corinthians 15.31 '*I die daily.*'

1 *A flexible timetable*

A holiday-maker in a remote and rural part of Southern Ireland was anxious to catch the local bus. He could find no sign of a timetable at the stop in the village square, although the bus was standing there, seemingly ready to go. When he enquired of a local inhabitant at what time the bus was expected to depart, the smilingly polite but cryptic reply was, 'Oh, most any time!' This was apparently true; when the driver and the people were ready, the bus left, and if he were not on board at that moment of common consent, it

1. Published in paperback by SPCK, 1962, p.17.

would be nobody's fault but his own. The potential passenger needed to have a personal timetable, sufficiently flexible for him to be on hand when the crucial moment came. Some people would take this to be a refreshingly 'laid back' approach to the art of living. Others with more demanding diaries would find it intolerable.

2 *Awaiting an invitation*

In our Lord's time, the experience of waiting for a forthcoming event, without knowing precisely when it would happen, was common enough for him to use it in more than one of his parables. He talked of the girls invited to be bridesmaids at a wedding, who must stand by for long hours until the bridegroom came; also of the bailiff left in charge of the rich man's estate, not knowing exactly when his master would return. Woe betide either of them if they were found unprepared when the crucial moment came! In the case of a big dinner-party like the one mentioned in the gospel, invitations would have been sent out and accepted long beforehand, indicating a day but not a specific time. Guests were expected to hold themselves ready to be summoned by a messenger when everything was ready. At that stage, to refuse an invitation previously accepted, however inconvenient the moment, would be seen as an insult to the host. From the midst of his tightly scheduled timetable, modern Western man might well complain of being kept kicking his heels. Oriental courtesy regarded the kind of personage who arranged a banquet as of too high a rank to be slighted.

3 *Optimists and pessimists*

Even so, there were three guests who, for private business and domestic reasons, turned down the final invitation, unwilling to break away from personal concerns to do honour to the host. Was it that at heart they were really pessimists? The mixture of patience and anticipation with which, in those days, people waited upon the coming of the bridegroom on the arrival of a messenger, reflects a basic optimism very similar to that of the rural Irishman – looking forward to the departure of the bus 'Oh, most any time' was said in a spirit of hopeful expectation, meaning that the crucial moment *would* come and, when it did, the passenger would be found ready and waiting.

Among the many joke definitions of 'optimist' and 'pessimist' is one from a small schoolgirl. 'An optimist', she said, 'is a person who looks after your eyes, and a pessimist is one who looks after your feet!' In a certain allegorical sense this schoolgirl 'howler' contains a grain of truth. An optimist is concerned with forward vision, seeing the potential good in situations and working towards it. A pessimist, by contrast, his eyes as it were cast down, sees no further than the feet plodding despondently along, forever afraid to break off or look up. The guests' refusal of the host's invitation reveals a lack of vision arising from a fearful self concern. How reluctant they were to break away from their ego-centred projects!

4 *Invitation to life*

The central message of the christian gospel is a call to strip away the false securities to which we cling in order to discover new life. At the birth of a baby there is a sense in which the mother cannot 'have' the child until she 'loses' it, that is, until she is separated from it. A writer will talk about 'throwing off' a poem or a book; it is there within him until he lets it go on to paper so that it can come alive both for him and his readers. The same principle applies to the work of an artist and a musician. Each act of detachment and surrender is, in a sense, a kind of death; but it is also an invitation to life. St Paul, in the fifteenth chapter of 1 Corinthians, bears witness to the power of Christ's resurrection and speaks, in verse 31, of his own 'dying' daily. The power of the resurrection can be ours here and now if we are prepared to accept the Lord's invitation to new life in him, but acceptance will involve facing these lesser deaths until we 'wear the likeness of the heavenly man' (verse 40, *NEB*). Waiting and watching for him day by day will enable us to savour every moment with expectancy and hope until the time of our departure for that heavenly banquet of love that knows no end.

PENTECOST 3

God as personality in relationship

Luke 8.44 (*NEB*) '*Jesus said "who was it that touched me?"*'

Any candidate for the Presidency of the United States must be prepared to shake innumerable hands. It was said of President Johnson during his campaign for re-election, that at the end of each day his right hand needed bathing and massaging, having been clasped by so many voters. Even so, of the crowds waiting for such a personal meeting with the President, the majority would be disappointed, for neither President nor Pope can shake hands with more than one person at a time. None of us has unlimited powers of attention. The whole world may be paraded before us by modern media of communication, but, because we are finite beings, only the tiniest part will ever engage us personally.

1 *Our personal and distinctive identity*

The old music-hall song brings the focus of attention down to the single person of the beloved: 'If you were the only girl in the world and I were the only boy, . . . Nothing else would matter in the world today . . .' For finite man the song betrays a selfish exclusiveness, but, for an infinite God, to give personal and undivided attention to all his children is perfectly possible. He treats me as if I were the only one in the world. Because he is God he can do this. No one less could bestow his love upon me as an individual, simultaneously, with every other one of his children. His love and his power are limitless, yet the identity of each one of us is distinctive and precious to him.

2 *Jesus 'at home' with the woman*

This experience of God as personality in relationship is revealed in the brief incident in the gospel when a woman in distress touches the hem of Jesus' cloak. The circumstances bear a vivid resemblance to a 'walk about' by one of today's VIPs, surrounded, but only partially protected, by a bodyguard. Central to the scene is Jesus, being hemmed in and pressed upon by the crowds, with the disciples in close attendance. The jostling throng accorded a merciful anonymity to the woman, who, because of her chronic affliction, believed herself to be an outcast. But she longed to be restored, and so, hoping not to be noticed or identified, she sought the momentary contact which she profoundly believed would cure her. She had no thought of a handshake, or of a personal meeting; she shrank from the embarrassment of a confrontation. Her aim was just to touch the very edge of his garment and then slip back into the faceless crowd.

She discovered, however, that it is impossible to reach out to Jesus, however fleetingly, without his knowing and responding. She received more than a cure – she was given acceptance and identity. To the disciples she was just another member of the crowd: to him, in that moment of recognition, it seemed as if no one but the woman, and nothing but her need, existed. He was, as they say, 'at home' with her.

3 *Not a statistic recorded but a person loved*

It is a rare and rewarding experience when someone is happy to be 'at home' with us, without haste or preoccupation. The security of such a relationship in contrast to the possessive idolization of 'the only girl in the world' reflects our Lord's readiness to take a personal interest in every one of his children. The society we live in needs to label us, to get us on to its computer as impersonal statistics. In an organizational age we are members of some social grouping before we are individuals; and if, because of our particular circumstances, we cannot be classified, then there is no place for us and we are pushed to the edge of the community.

From the margins of a society which regarded her as ceremonially unclean, the woman came trembling to the feet of our Lord, and out of that poignant encounter comes a message to be heard by us all.

It is not the message of the mighty potentate, generous in victory: 'God is all powerful and can surely find room even for you'. It is the message of the suffering redeemer, identified in his life and death with the weak and powerless of any society: 'God loves you *and* everyone else; he suffers for you and with you, his individual child'. It is to this God we may dare to entrust ourselves, day by day.

PENTECOST 4

Lost and found

> Luke 15.10 (*RSV*) '*There is joy before the angels of God over one sinner who repents.*'

The popular jargon of twentieth century culture has produced some vivid and sometimes unprintable ways of telling someone to go away. These expressions are usually curt and monosyllabic, like the American 'scram', coined in the days of gangsterdom and Prohibition. In our day, the same sentiment is chillingly conveyed in the two short words 'Get lost!' It would be difficult to think of a more brutal form of rejection than to be consigned to the place where there is no location or direction – the place of 'lostness'.

1 *Two parables*

Today's gospel reminds us that 'lostness' can come by chance rather than through banishment or rejection, but it is devastatingly desolate either way. In the parables of the lost sheep and of the lost coin, Jesus makes appeal to our imagination as he brings the scenes to life. We can almost hear the lonely sheep bleating plaintively on the mountain-side, and see with our mind's eye the glint of the solitary silver coin concealed in a dark corner under the straw. The sheep, without looking up from its grazing, has nibbled its random way into isolation. The coin, having been dropped, has hit the floor and rolled by its own momentum into its hiding place. Both of them are separated from the group to which they rightly belong; how then are they to be retrieved from their lostness?

Again we can picture the scene in imagination: the shepherd setting out on his quest equipped with both rod and staff – the former iron-tipped and cut down to a handy size for warding off attack, the latter firm for support on the journey and for reaching out to guide the wayward member of the flock. It may be that, in the mountainous terrain of the wilderness, the sheep has got itself stuck on a ledge from which it cannot retreat and dare not go on. Whatever scene we may visualize as the setting for either of the two parables, the same point is made in both. Just as the lost sheep is unable to rescue itself and needs the shepherd's aid, so the lost coin cannot find itself but has to be hidden until it is unearthed from its dark recess by the householder, with the aid of a lamp and a broom.

2 *Joyful celebration*

The initial emphasis in both stories is upon the eagerness of the respective owners to go out of their way to search for what has been missing. The sequel, when the lost are found, is a joyful celebration. The neighbours are invited in to rejoice with them at being reunited with their own. What a contrast there is in their outgoing joy from the negative and vindictive attitude of the man, who, not casually, but with real antagonism, tells another to 'Get lost'!

3 *Three parables*

The parables of the wayward sheep and the wayward coin are part of a series of three which make up the fifteenth chapter of Luke. The third is about a wayward son who wanders to a far country from which he must needs return in order to be reunited with his father. Each part of the trilogy culminates in joyful celebration, having first revealed the process by which the wandering one is brought back from the place of lostness to the place of belonging. The sheep has to be redirected into the right path, the coin to be retrieved from solitary darkness, the Prodigal, in his isolation, to turn about and head for home. Jesus builds up these parallel images around the process of rescue to which he finally gives a name – 'repentance'.

4 *Repentance and rescue*

At every act of christian initiation the question is put to the candidates or to their godparents, 'Do you repent of your sins?' It is worth considering, against a secular background in which the words 'sin' and 'sinner' have largely been emptied of meaning, whether that question should be reinterpreted, 'Do you recognize your need to be rescued?' Repentance is that moment of insight in which we know both that we have lost our way and that rescue is possible. Apparently, the whole of heaven gives itself to merrymaking when just one person comes to that moment of recognition.

'This man', said the Pharisees, in a cutting indictment of Jesus, 'receives sinners and eats with them.' Yet there was joy among those who sat with him at table. Still he seeks his own, eager to draw them to feast with him, and rejoices with the angels when the lost ones allow him to find them.

PENTECOST 5

A Church in mission

> Luke 10.2 (*NEB*) '*The crop is heavy but the labourers are few. You must therefore beg the owner to send labourers to harvest his crop.*'

The campaign to preserve the English churchyard as a habitat for wildlife is not without its opponents. Conservationists sometimes find themselves in contention with conscientious churchwardens and other custodians of 'God's acre', who have a vision of their church and its environs as a diamond set down upon a cloth of green velvet; the greensward neatly trimmed, with neat rows of gravestones standing clear of weeds or undergrowth. Both points of view can be justified by local circumstance. Where graveyards are still in use for burial, there is clearly an obligation to tend them decently, but where large-scale farming methods have regimented the landscape, disposing of the hedgerows, the local churchyard can come into its own as an unofficial nature reserve.

1 *The fields white to harvest*

At harvest festival time, when the fruits of the earth are being marshalled into orderly and beautiful arrangements, there are some enlightened church decorators ready to leave space for a 'wilderness windowsill' of wild flowers and grasses, signifying that unruly abundance of nature not to be found in cultivated suburban gardens. By bringing the wild profusion of nature into a well-ordered church interior, and letting it appear over and against the neat rows of pews and kneelers, they offer a reminder of where our Lord's ministry and mission began. Although he regularly took part in the structured worship of the temple, his call to ministry came in the wilderness, and the beginnings of his mission in the open countryside. 'The fields are white to harvest',[1] he said

1. John 4.35.

as he looked upon the swarming, white-garmented crowds drawn by his all inclusive invitation to enter the Kingdom. This harvest would come from the seed of the gospel, broadcast prodigally; not in neatly drilled rows, but right across the boundaries of social, religious and political class structures. It is from that vital proclamation, directed towards all mankind, that the Church derives its essential character as a church in mission. The vision we are given in today's gospel is one of urgency for the harvest to be gathered while it is ripe and teeming. Can we, in today's Church, fulfil that vision?

2 *'Go' structures*

When we come to consider the congregational life of the majority of churches in our society, we find that they are based on what a World Council of Churches' Report[2] once referred to as 'come' structures. By this was meant that all their activities of worship and fellowship would be centred upon the church buildings, and that mission, such as it was, would be thought of in terms of drawing outsiders in to share these concerns. The nature of mission as revealed by Jesus seems to require 'Go' structures, if his commission to 'send labourers to harvest the crop' is to be obeyed. Our inherited patterns of church life and worship serve to build up and to nourish the faith of those who come in, but if a church, however well ordered and organized, has no means of witnessing *to* the world, *in* the world, it ceases to function as a church in mission. 'Your love', said one American preacher, 'has a broken wing if it cannot fly across the sea.'[3]

3 *The village evangelists*

How can we learn to engage in mission in ways that will reveal Christ's all-inclusive love to modern man? The

2. See *God for all men* by Robert Latham, (Edinburgh House Press).
3. Maltbie D. Babcock.

experience of the seventy-two sent out by Jesus as 'village evangelists' teaches us three truths about their missionary strategy which may help to shape and renew our own approach.

Firstly, they went out precariously, without any reserves of money, food or clothes. So precariously! And yet, in the context of mission, their lack of accustomed securities was only one side of the coin. The other was dependence; dependence upon the Lord and upon those prepared to hear them and to give them hospitality. Mission is not regarding your neighbour as the object of your 'do-gooding'. It is being so filled with a sense of your own inadequacy that you are open to be filled with the Lord's strength and compassion.

Secondly, they went out in pairs and not alone. They had to involve themselves with one another from the start so that they could represent, by their fellowship, the whole interdependence of human existence.

And finally, they went out, not with any particular theory of mission, but with great joy; conscious only of the certainty of being loved and sustained by the one who had commissioned them.

4 *His grace is sufficient*

Reflecting upon this model of mission with its implications for today's Church, we may, at first, experience a deep sense of inadequacy and failure. But any human failure is as nothing compared with the abundance of the grace of Christ. When we return to the source of grace, we shall come to recognize that the mission to the teeming world in which we live is not ours, but his. As we respond to his call to share in it, so he will show us new ways of developing in obedience to that call. We shall refuse to be immobilized by our neat and orderly securities, and we shall be ready to be gloriously overrun by the new life flooding into the Kingdom.

PENTECOST 6

A summons to salvation

Mark 10.47 (*NEB*) '*Hearing that it was Jesus of Nazareth, he began to shout, Son of David, Jesus have pity on me.*'

1 *A hasty construction*

We begin with a brief glimpse into the case history of a man living in sixteenth century England. Not a man of 'gentle' birth or a member of the prosperous yeoman class, but one of the labouring poor, accustomed to working on arable land. With the rise of the increasingly profitable wool trade, he has been driven out of both his home and his livelihood and is desperate to provide at least a roof for his family. Word has come to him of an ancient right to which he can lay claim, together with a prompting to act quickly before the inevitable change in the law. By this entitlement a man could build a house on common land so long as the roof was raised and a fire burning in the grate before sunset, having started at dawn on same day. It would have to be a hasty construction of sticks and mud but, for the destitute labourer, it could be a first step towards salvaging his future, whilst many of his contemporaries, not as well placed to seize the opportunity, would continue in ignorance and poverty.

2 *Waiting and wanting*

Let me come back to the twentieth century and remind you of the promotional slogan associated with the first issue of a certain credit card, which claimed that it took 'the waiting out of wanting'. A piece of persuasive advertizing aimed at a relatively prosperous society avid for quick returns. In less affluent or competitive societies, advertizing of this kind is totally irrelevant. (Who needs to advertize bread during a famine?) For those modern counterparts of our Elizabethan labourer in all the underprivileged parts of the globe, the last syllable of the credit card catchphrase needs to be docked. What they are looking for is an agency to take 'the waiting out of *want*'.

There has been no shortage in recent years of publicity for the plight of the oppressed and depressed peoples of the world. The voices of many agencies have clamoured on behalf of the hungry and the homeless. Speeches have been made at the United Nations, reports have been produced, endless conferences held and still there are thousands who continue to wait in want. Their cry of need, even if heard, is apparently not welcome in the centres of power and prosperity.

3 *A roadside healing*

The gospel gives us a brief glimpse into the case history of someone whose cry of need was undoubtedly heard, but among the group centred upon Jesus on the road out of Jericho, it was certainly not welcome. Bartimeus had been driven, by the combination of poverty with blindness, into begging at the roadside. When word came to him that Jesus was approaching, his cry was clamorous and insistent. 'Jesus, have pity on me'; and they rebuked him for it. 'Hold your tongue', they said; and they might have added, 'What has your ignorance and poverty to do with the Rabbi?'

There is a Chinese proverb which reminds us that a journey of a thousand miles begins with one step. The cry of the blind beggar prompted by need and opportunity was his first step towards healing and discipleship, and the attitude of Jesus stands in contrast to that of the group around him. Even though his face is set now towards Jerusalem and the road out of Jericho is the road to the cross, he turns aside to give his whole attention to this final miracle of healing.

We, who claim to be a group centred on Jesus, are challenged by this brief and dramatic encounter on the road. It calls into question our own feelings and attitudes. When we hear a cry of need, whether from nearby or far away, what does our response reveal? Is it saying, like the crowd, 'Hold your tongue', or is it reflecting the positive, accepting attitude of our Lord? And if, as we enter by our imagination into the gospel scene, we find ourselves identifying with Bartimeus in his cry for mercy, will it be for us, as it was for him, a step along the Jesus road? And can we handle the fact that on that road there is no easy way around the cross?

There was an immediacy about the response of Bartimeus to the news of Jesus' approach, which is echoed in the instant house-building of the sixteenth century peasant. Both of them were at the bottom of the social pile, their voices pitifully insignificant but their readiness to grasp at the passing opportunity an example to reflect upon. 'If you take one step towards God he will take ten steps towards you', says an Indian proverb. That step cannot be taken in the past which is behind us, and if we try to postpone it to the future that special moment of progress is lost. It is *now*, at the very present stage of our life's journey, by the roadside, that God summons us to salvation.

PENTECOST 7

Hearing and listening

Deuteronomy 6.4a '*Hear O Israel . . .*'

'You have been given two ears but one mouth. Therefore listen twice as much as you speak.'

This ancient precept is rarely observed in contemporary life, scourged as it is by a continual barrage of noise, much of which issues from the amplified human voice. Mouths would appear to be working overtime, whilst ears are being deafened and so debarred from their true function.

1 *The hearing process*

The pity of it is that, among all the organs of the human body, the ear is one of the most sensitive. A simple diagram of its structure shows it to be in three sections. On the outside there is a funnel or trumpet picking up a whole medley of sounds from near and far. These pass along to the eardrum, the clearing house for the delicate nerve centre of the inner ear where signals are selected and passed to the brain. A complex operation of shifting and discarding is thus involved in the process of hearing.

The ancient Hebrews, knowing nothing of these intricate mechanisms, still regarded the ear as vital to the whole being. For them, the total person was involved in the hearing process so that the ear became the organ of response and obedience. It is not easy for us in an environment which is, as it were, 'wallpapered' with sound on all sides, to achieve that level of full and exclusive attention whereby the whole self is concentrated in the act of hearing. It can come unbidden in rare moments: a moment of alarm in the quiet of the night when an unfamiliar sound alerts us to the possibility of an intruder; a profound moment during a concert when 'we are the music while the music lasts'. In these situations our whole attention and response are exercised via the ear.

2 *The 'Shema'*

To experience such moments is to be given an insight into the basic confession of faith of every pious jew, the *Shema* quoted by our Lord to the lawyer in today's gospel. The word means 'Hear' and comes from the first and great commandment beginning 'Hear O Israel . . .'. Twice a day it was to be recited, reminding the worshipper that, through the faculty of hearing, his whole being stood in relationship to God. 'Hear O Israel': the Lord our God is the only Lord and *you shall love the Lord your God with all your heart, with all your soul, with all your mind, and with all your strength.*

3 *Spiritual deafness*

The response of love that hearing demands cannot be partial or fragmented. Have you noticed the symbol of physical deafness appearing in a number of high street shop windows where facilities for the hard of hearing are available? It can provide us with a simple parable for our time. The sign shows a stylized outer ear with a broad band cutting across it. Let it challenge our spiritual deafness and convey the truth that, when we hear and respond only partially to God, we threaten the unity of our whole personality. Hardness of spiritual hearing can lead to hardness of heart.

Anthony de Mello, in his anthology of stories *The Song of the Bird*, offers us the following soliloquy:

> I used to be stone deaf. I would see people stand up and go through all kinds of gyrations. They called it dancing. It looked absurd to me . . . until one day I heard the music,

and the author appends a comment, also in the first person:

> I fail to understand why saints – and lovers – behave the way they do. So I'm waiting for my heart to come alive.

4 *A listening attitude*

Another modern parable is presented to us by the physical construction of the human ear in its sensitive process of receiving and selecting.

It may be helpful, in this context, to draw a distinction between hearing and listening. We hear the clamour of our modern culture, but do we really listen to its underlying message? We hear the neighbour, the friend, the colleague, but is their deepest need being interpreted by our inner ear? The christian is called to listen to people as one might listen intensely to music, seeking to catch the subtle harmonies below the surface melody.

God will speak by his Spirit to that deepest inner ear of intuition and understanding if only we will put ourselves into a listening attitude. The sign that we have truly received what the Spirit is saying to us will be in the response of love and obedience which follows upon our hearing.

PENTECOST 8

Identity and community

> Luke 6.38 (*NEB*) '*Give, and gifts will be given you. Good measure pressed down, shaken together, and running over . . . for whatever measure you deal out to others will be dealt out to you in return.*'

1 *Thanks for the memory*

Something has happened to memory. The era of romantic nostalgia, evoked by the lyrics of the old songwriters, has been overtaken by high technology. In our present pragmatic culture it has become tabulated and depersonalized. Computers have memory banks; calculators and word processors retain information for instant recall; even the domestic telephone can nowadays be equipped to memorize data and reproduce it to order. One of the consequences of this robotic approach to remembering has been a sharp rise in the value of memorabilia. Anything with a claim to be labelled 'vintage', from motor cars to medicine bottles, commands a price that would have amazed the generation for whom these things were merely commonplace.

2 *Going back to the roots*

Although the perfecting of artificial electronic memory represents a genuine advance in one area of human need, modern man still searches for richer and deeper ways of recalling the past. The recent crop of articles, exhibitions and television programmes dealing with some aspect of archaeology or tribalism represents a fascination for the elemental and the primitive. If we are to find our true place in the order of things, we need to know that we are part of a story – a continuity of meaning which exposes the hidden substructure linking us with the rest of creation.

The ancient Israelite, bringing his basket of first-fruits to the altar, stood before the priest and recited the time-honoured story which gave identity to him and to his people.[1] He recounted with pride their deliverance from Egypt and entry into the Promised Land, not as a piece of historical data but as a confession of faith. This offering of himself and his gift within the context of a story was part of a living tradition; it located him firmly in the religious and social structures binding the tribe together. Imagine a great choir and orchestra performing some major work, voices and instruments blending in glorious harmony, and you have a symbol of the primitive communal life of ancient Israel known as the *shalom*. It was a dynamic network of contribution in which there were no extremes of wealth or poverty and everyone had sufficient for their needs. Its members lived in dependence on God and on each other in the kind of existence which allowed no possibility of greed or excess.

3 *Wisdom that stirs the heart*

The ancient wisdom of the *shalom* is reflected in the teaching of Jesus, and yet is radically re-interpreted by him. Ancient Israel prohibits murder, Jesus denounces anger; it

1 Deuteronomy 26.1–11.

forbids adultery, Jesus condemns adulterous thoughts; it sanctions equal retaliation for injury, Jesus vetoes any form of revenge; in the Old Testament communities a neighbour was a fellow Israelite, but according to Christ he could be anybody, even an enemy.

The precepts set out in today's gospel are not to be received as we might take in facts from a computer screen; if we attempt to interpret them by intellect alone we shall be put off by their apparent impracticability. They are not so much to be understood literally as to be listened to, the way we listen to great music or poetry, allowing it to take us out of the functional level of our being – which feeds only on information – and to awaken the imagination. In this way our heart is stirred and our will is given direction. These sayings are all of a piece with the stories that follow them in the sixth chapter of St Luke: simple parables of common life about removing a speck from a brother's eye, or picking fruit, or laying the foundations of a house. God's presence is associated with the events of everyday experience by the telling of stories. These, too, touch us deeply and mysteriously in a part of our being that is beyond intelligence.

Modern man, with his micro-chip memory, faces the danger of being tyrannized by instant information. If he is to escape, he must recover a sense of the great spiritual landscape in which he is placed. He is not able, like the traditional jew, to locate his identity in a tribal memory, but he still has the events of everyday life from which, if he will, he can draw parables of ultimate meaning.

4 *A holiday snapshot*

Let us end with one such tiny incident – a kind of holiday snapshot to illustrate the poetic words of the text with which we began.

Two children were playing one day on the beach; one was eight years old, the other five, and the respective sizes of their buckets and spades represented the difference in their ages.

'Your bucket can't hold anything', said the bigger child with great scorn.

'Perhaps it doesn't hold much', was the quick reply, 'but it can overflow lots.'

Out of the mouths of these innocents come wisdom. Our opportunities in life may be restricted, our minds of limited capacity to take in unlimited facts, but we can 'overflow lots' in daily acts of giving and forgiving. Blessed are they of whom it can be said that, according to their capacity, they overflow with love; for such folk reveal something of what God is like.

PENTECOST 9

From 'faith' to 'faith in'

Mark 9.24 (*NEB*) '*I have faith . . . help me where faith falls short.*'

1 *It's all a gamble*

Just a few yards from the parish church in a small country town, and next door to the local post office, stood the betting shop. The close proximity of these three gave rise to a good deal of satirical humour among the townspeople. There were jokes about those who drew money from the Post Office only to lose it all in the establishment next door; and cynical comparisons between one lot of folk who were ready to put their trust in a particular racehorse and the other lot who went a few steps further along to invest it in religion. 'What's the difference?' demanded the quipsters; 'You have a certain amount of slender evidence to go on and then you make an act of faith. It's all a gamble anyway!'

2 *Two thresholds*

One answer to their cynical questioning might have been to point out that the punter, having crossed the threshold of the betting shop, does not then have to take the further step of believing that the object of his faith exists: he can be reasonably certain that the race card is accurate. All he gambles upon is the reliability of the horse he has chosen after weighing up the evidence of the form book and the tipsters. For the aspiring christian, however, there are two thresholds to cross. First, he must take the step of faith that God exists, and then the much greater step of trust and confidence that this God is to be relied upon. The second threshold moves him from 'faith' to 'faith in'; it is a matter of personal commitment; we might liken it to the difference between accepting the evidence of a brass name-plate indicating that a doctor is available, and actually calling that doctor out and obeying his or her instructions when one's child is critically ill.

The evidence at hand to take us across the first threshold is not so slender. The story of Israel, Jesus of Nazareth, and the emergence of his Church is enough to bring us to a responsible choice. Few people, even today, will confess to being outright atheists, but so many stop short, content with a hazy acceptance of the existence of 'God' which evokes no response in worship or action. Faith (and it is doubtful whether such an attitude deserves the name at all) needs conviction and effort to become 'faith *in*'. The gambler who is prepared to put a substantial wager upon his conviction is a salutary example. The chosen horse – among all the rival possibilities in the field – has, by virtue of the portion of his capital investment in it, become the one to which he is personally committed. Faith has become faith *in*.

3 *A lifelong process*

Christian believers, having taken the initial step of acknowledging the existence of God, will discover that crossing the second threshold whereby they are able to profess 'I believe and trust *in* him', is a lifelong and continual process. There can never be a moment in our life of faith when we are able to claim that we have 'arrived' – that our faith is a finished product. The heart-cry of the father of the epileptic boy in today's gospel expresses our own sense of inadequacy: 'I have faith, help me where faith falls short'. Like a compulsive gambler, we are to return again and again to put our personal substance behind our belief, even against apparently overwhelming odds. There will be the good times when the everyday world is transfigured for us by glimpses of glory, and there will be the times of adversity when it requires an act of naked will to hold on to the reality of God in our lives. We do well to remember, when we are tempted to doubt and despair, that it was the presence of Christ in the valley, and not on the mount of Transfiguration, which saved the epileptic boy. Just a few steps along the path of sincere enquiry can bring us to the step of rational acceptance. Beyond that, the reason and the will must go hand in hand across the second threshold to faith in the dependence upon the God whom we have accepted. Many times we shall hear an echo in our own experience of the cry from the gospel, but perhaps – as the Authorized Version puts it – in its starkest form: 'Lord I believe; help thou mine unbelief'. Holding firm to our commitment at those times of crisis serves to strengthen and deepen our faith. No greater doubt or darkness can fall upon us than fell upon our Lord at the cross. It was there that he made a total commitment of himself and won the total victory which is the basis of all our believing.

PENTECOST 10

The joy of sin forgiven

Luke 7.47 (*NEB*) '*Where little has been forgiven, little love is shown.*'

1 *Upstairs Downstairs*

Why was the television serial 'Upstairs Downstairs' so popular? Given that it was well acted and carefully produced, what was it about the dramatized story of an Edwardian household above and below stairs that captivated such a wide audience? Part of the attraction, as with any period piece, lay in the view it gave of the background to a vanished lifestyle, but the main interest was surely in the storyline. Having revealed the rigidly hierarchical structures obtaining both in the drawing room and in the servants' quarters, the plot was chiefly concerned with the interaction between the various levels of authority. It was easy to see how a threat to the order and stability of the system might come from anyone who had 'ideas above their station'. Rules of precedence were rigorously applied to entertaining. Among the upper echelons of society an invitation to a formal dinner party carried with it an obligation to observe strict protocol. How easy to be compromised over a meal table! How dangerous to flout the etiquette of hospitality!

2 *In conflict with convention*

A social system determined to keep all of its classes within the strict boundaries assigned to them is not unique to the Edwardian era. There are harshly administered examples of it in our own day, as there were in the ancient world. Jesus constantly found himself in potentially dangerous conflict with the conventions of his society, particularly among the religious hierarchy. Simon the Pharisee, who invited him to dinner, treated him with cool and formal politeness; very much as a haughty Edwardian hostess might have dealt with a member of the lower orders. None of the customary courtesies were extended to him, the feet washing, and kiss of greeting and the anointing of his head with fragrant oil. It was made perfectly clear by the patronizing attitude of the host that the name of Jesus of Nazareth was low down on a fashionable guest list. Simon, who applied codified laws of behaviour towards certain classes of people, was due to be scandalized!

It is worth, for a moment, picturing the scene: the meal, probably taking place in the open courtyard at the centre of the villa, the guests reclining on couches, their bare feet stretched out behind them. The doors left open to allow passers-by to wander in and hear (at a respectful distance) the conversation of the intelligentsia. And one of those who came in was a woman of doubtful reputation who clearly had 'ideas above her station'. Not only did she anoint and kiss the feet of Jesus, she took the unpardonable liberty, for a jewish woman, of letting down her hair to wipe away her tears. Simon was appalled; not only by her behaviour, but most especially by Jesus' acknowledgement and acceptance of her. 'If this man were a prophet', he said to himself, 'he would know who this woman is that is touching him, and what a bad name she has.'

3 *Sins and sins*

In that muttered indictment we hear a voice which is painfully familiar to many of us in our own situation. It is the loveless voice of the one who is wholly self-satisfied; the joyless voice of the one who hates to be indebted or beholden. We then know that, like the Pharisee, we have not yet understood the depth and extent of what God is offering us when he forgives us. It is something so much more than the wiping clean of a scribbled slate of wrongs. Our sins (with a small 's') are only boils on the skin betraying the poison in the bloodstream. Sin (with a capital 'S') is nothing less than a falling short of that perfection of love to which Christ calls us (Matt. 5.48). The attitude of our Lord, in bringing liberation from outdated conventions and overthrowing tight barriers of oppression, creates a climate of acceptance and forgiveness. In it we can, like the woman in the gospel, find our way back to God, even weeping, for such tears are tears of love and joy.

The opening prayer of the Eucharist, the Collect for Purity, draws us with her to the feet of Christ, and invites us to 'let our hair down' before the Lord 'to whom all hearts are open, all desires known, and from whom no secrets are hidden.' It is not bidding us to concentrate upon the gulf between what we are and what he would have us be, for that way lies nagging guilt. It is calling us to be cleansed so that we may 'perfectly love him and worthily magnify his holy Name'.

PENTECOST 11

The generous employer

> Proverbs 2.2 (*RSV*) '*Making your ear attentive to wisdom and inclining your heart to understanding.*'

Let us begin with a quotation from a great preacher, Edward Caird, late Master of Balliol College, Oxford, delivering a sermon to his undergraduates. 'We are apt to forget', he told them, 'that life masks its great issues under the appearance of a series of unimportant circumstances and events, in each of which however, there is some opportunity for the exercise of courage or cowardice, truthfulness or untruthfulness, magnanimity or meanness, justice or injustice, charity or uncharitableness, love or hate.'[1]

1 *A feud resolved*

Most of life's routine is made up of what Caird refers to elsewhere in his sermon as 'the little exigencies of every day', yet the way some of these are resolved can bear a weight that supports the truth of his words.

Take an English village, where in the post-war period there was a petty feud going on between the Village Hall Committee and the Parochial Church Council. The parish and the diocese in question must remain anonymous, although the situation as it is described may sound all too familiar! Since the completion of the new hall, the P.C.C.

From *Lay Sermons delivered in Balliol College*, Caird.

had made regular use of the building for Sunday School classes, socials and various other gatherings, because it possessed no meeting place of its own. Consequently, at the beginning of the financial year, there was invariably a wrangle over the question of whether these activities merited a concessionary tariff or not. The full hire charge in operation at that time, of fifty pounds for the year, sounds a paltry amount today; nevertheless the Church Council devoted almost the whole of one session to a heated protest against it. The meeting was being chaired by the new vicar, who, having listened long and patiently to the debate, quietly interjected a suggestion: 'Why not pay them double?' There was a shocked silence in which the emotional atmosphere of the meeting shifted from indignation via incredulity to a dawning realization that the vicar meant what he said. His paradoxical remark was to be taken seriously. Further discussion ensued, ending in a resolution that the treasurer should draw a cheque in favour of the village hall for one hundred pounds!

2 *A different kind of wisdom*

From that day forward, relations between the two committees were on an entirely different basis; each responding to the other according to its needs rather than to what had been judged to be its deserts. A different kind of wisdom had been brought into play; godly wisdom. Worldly wisdom had originally prompted a perfectly fair and reasonable attempt to achieve as economic a rate as possible. We cannot live without worldly wisdom; books have to be balanced and well-planned budgets are important. But neither can we live with worldly wisdom alone, as the story in today's gospel makes clear.

3 *Wage slaves or partners?*

The parable of the 'Labourers in the Vineyard' or – as it might be more aptly entitled – 'The Generous Employer' goes against the grain of worldly wisdom. Indeed, it seems to threaten the primary principle of equal pay for equal work upon which much of the fabric of industrial relations is founded. A just reward, according to the wage-packet grumblers in the parable, had not been received. By treating them at the level of godly wisdom, however, the Employer endowed them with the status of partners in his enterprise. None of them had started with anything of his own. It was only by the generosity of the Employer that they obtained any work or any reward whatsoever. He was the source of all that they had received.

4 *Response to loving wisdom*

The truth we are being offered as we hear this parable is reflected in the attitude of the Generous Employer. It is a truth about the nature of God. He is the source of all our being. There is nothing that we have, nothing that we are which we did not receive from him. As the realization of the fact that all my life is a gift dawns upon me I have to ask, what is to be my response? An endless wrangle over differentials? A rebellion against his generosity in causing the sun to shine on the just and the unjust? A murmuring at the apparently unmerited prosperity of certain of my neighbours? The mighty paradoxes of godly wisdom, so hard for the world to understand, are scattered through the gospels from the lips of our Lord –

> 'Love your enemies, do good to those who hate you' (Luke 6.28).
>
> 'Whoever will save his life shall lose it, whoever will lose his life for my sake shall find it' (Mark 8.35, 36).
>
> 'Do good and lend without expecting any return and you will have a rich reward' (Luke 6.35).

He calls us in the apparently humdrum round of daily life to respond to his loving wisdom; not with a surface reaction, pretending a claim to what we think should be ours, but in the depths of our heart's understanding as we are confronted by each event and circumstance. As we begin to do this we shall know what it is to be partners in his great enterprise.

PENTECOST 12

The light of Christ

Matthew 5.16 (*JB*) '. . . *Your light must shine in the sight of men* . . .'

1 *Our vocation to bear light*

How disruptive to the smooth running of any household is a sudden power cut; especially if it happens during a peak period on a winter's evening! In the midst of a world of advanced technology able to project lasers into space and to illuminate whole cities at the touch of a switch, the benighted householder is left groping bleakly for candles and matches. It is the kind of predicament that can bring us closer to the experience of our forefathers who depended for illumination upon oil lamps or wax candles and heard the cry of the watchman ringing through their streets as darkness was falling 'Hang out your lights'. With the coming of automation, the provision of light is no longer an individual responsibility. The day of the street lamp lighter is long past: soon, we are told, the lighthouse keeper will follow him down the road of redundancy.

In terms of the gospel, however, there remains for the Church and for the individual christian, a clear vocation to be bearers of light. It is as if we hear a call addressed to us in a darkening world 'Hang out your lights'. How are we to interpret and to act upon that call?

2 *Two images of light*

It may help briefly to explore something of what is meant in scripture by the idea of light. The biblical writers use it to convey the effect of God's presence and power upon his people. We might compare it to a silken rope made up of two bright strands which are impossible to separate, so closely are they interwoven. One strand is a literal image, the other is a metaphor, showing us that the physical radiance of God is all of a piece with his goodness and holiness. The glory that shone around the Bethlehem shepherds and dazzled the disciples on the amount of Transfiguration is at one with a divine inner light not visible to the naked eye. Who better than St Paul to describe the source and nature of that light? Listen to the way he weaves the two strands together, 'It is the God who said "Let light shine out of darkness" who has shone in our hearts to give us the light of the knowledge of the glory of God in the face of Jesus Christ.' (2 Corinthians 4.6 *RSV*).

3 *The creative word*

High above the north doorway of the great cathedral at Chartres among the many figures adorning the central arch is a small but exquisitely carved sculpture of the creation of Adam. A casual observer would miss both its beauty and its truth, but the one prepared to focus on it with binoculars could make a discovery that brings home the full import of St Paul's words. *The sculptor has given the creator the face of Christ.*

The creative word providing the daylight by which Adam and all his creatures can see and walk, is made flesh in Jesus. He is the source of light at work in the world from the very beginning. Those who believe in him are called children of light (Ephesians 5.8) because they have passed out of heathen darkness. The mightly symbolism of light overcoming darkness is there whenever a new christian is baptized or 'Christ-ened'. (How strikingly accurate is the popular word!) A new lamp is being lit from his inextinguishable light so that it may shine out in witness and service.

4 *The nature of our calling*

We have heard again in today's gospel Christ's eternal commission to his disciples to let their light shine in the sight of men. We do well to ask just how, in our particular situation, we propose to respond to that charge in the face of all the confusion and complexity of modern life, both within the Church and outside it. In every age there have been threats and hindrances to christian witness, never more perhaps than in our own. We need to be recalled constantly to the true nature of our calling.

We are not being summoned to the burdensome work of arguing people into faith. Our task is not so much to explain Christ as to show him to the world; to allow the light of his love, which has been kindled within us, to shine through. He will never be glorified by what we try to do in our own strength; an evangelism of self-assertion will blind people rather than illuminate them and will drive them back into comfortable darkness. It is by the constant patient practice of prayer and stillness, the daily nourishment of reading the scriptures and by worship and sacrament that we return again and again to the source of light which is Christ himself.

In the first epistle of John we are reminded that no man has seen God at any time (Ephesians 5.8). The only thing he *has* seen to convince or to convert him, is a person or a group of people whose whole personality and lifestyle has been transformed and is radiant with the light of Christ.

PENTECOST 13

True discipleship

Matthew 10.16 (*JB*) '. . . *harmless as doves.*'

1 *Arms, armour and bicycles*

A psychiatrist was lecturing a class of social work students on disorders of the personality. 'some of the people you are likely to meet in the course of your work may be compared to tanks', he said, using a military metaphor. 'You will find it hard to get through to them, either because of the thickness of their emotional armour or because of the heavy guns of rage and resentment with which they will keep you at bay.' 'As for you,' he continued, 'your role is more like that of a bicycle. Even army bikes can hardly be armed or armour-plated, neither must you be unduly aggressive or over-defensive.'

Harmless as bicycles? Surely those students, when they came to be confronted with the harsh realities of life in the field, must have dismissed this as a counsel of perfection. Selfish assertiveness and the rule of force dictate the fashion of the age; even the BMX machine ridden by a ten-year-old, complete with crash helmet and protective cladding, conforms to the popular 'macho' image. So much for the bicycle as a symbol of non-aggression!

The idea of confronting the world in a spirit of innocence and simplicity, claiming no rights and having no private defences, cuts clean across the conventions and assumptions of our time. This is nothing new. We hear in today's gospel how Jesus commissioned those he sent out into an arrogantly pagan world: they were to be as harmless as those archetypal symbols of non-aggression, doves.

2 *The world's reaction*

Allegiance to Christ in the first century carried a threat of persecution and possible martyrdom: the very name 'christian' during the reign of Nero was sufficient warrant for the death sentence. If the original reaction to christian discipleship was hostile, how does it fare in the last decades of the twentieth century?

There are parts of the world where the view that God does not exist is officially promulgated by the state, and where believers are liable to be discriminated against. Even in countries where the national Church is nominally christian, as in South America, men and women in active ministry in the name of Christ have suffered rejection and abuse. Heroic and heart-warming stories of christian witness in the face of persecution have emerged from these places in recent years. None the less, the world as a whole carries on its power-struggles without offering to christians the ruthless opposition encountered by the early Church. A christian commitment to live vulunerably, claiming no privileges or protection and possessing no worldly power, merely invites the cynical rejoinder, 'And having no backbone either!' 'Harmless' will be interpreted by the world at large as 'spineless'.

3 *Blandly inoffensive*

We have to face the fact that the image of irrelevancy and escapism which the Church has acquired in some quarters is largely deserved. Like a fragile bicycle removed from the roaring traffic of the main highway to its own secluded track, it has withdrawn onto a path of its own where real problems are evaded and self-preservation is paramount. This is a caricature of the harmlessness referred to in the gospel, a model for the music-hall parson with his vacuous smile and mincing gait. 'Harmless' has all to often been interpreted by the Church as 'blandly inoffensive'.

4 *The implications of involvement*

Can the Lord's doves survive amid the sophisticated weaponry of the modern world? Not if they are the tamed and domesticated variety! These are a dying breed. The call of Christ is not to remain aloof from the world's conflict but to stand where he stands, within it, involved with its pain and its needs. As we search for ways of being true to our discipleship in our own situation, let us remember the analogies of the doves and the bicycles and reflect upon their implications. Firstly, those who profess and call themselves christians should be constantly wary of power. We do not need it to give us identity, for God himself will safeguard our rights. Secondly, christians, like doves, are not to be domineering or defensive, but neither are they to be weak and foolish. Our business is to be peacemakers at the focus of conflict, absorbing its rage and resentment but never passing it on. And finally, apart from those periods of retreat and withdrawal vital to their spiritual wellbeing, christians must remain 'at the coalface', in touch with the real world. 'The Church is her true self only when she exists for humanity', wrote Dietriech Bonhoeffer.[1] May we rediscover what it means to live by this truth.

PENTECOST 14

A working standard

Luke 11.4b (*JB*) '*Do not put us to the test.*'

1 *Sounds familiar!*

Familiarity does not always breed contempt; occasionally the converse is true. Long familiarity with traditional forms of worship, for example, can engender loyalty and devotion, especially when changes are being proposed. There is a body of conservative opinion among church worshippers whose regard for old and well-tried ways is aptly expressed as 'knowing what they like and liking what they know': was it

1. *Letters and Papers from Prison*, Fontana Publications, chapter 3, line 1 of section entitled 'Outline for a book'.

the voice of tradition, I wonder, which influenced the final decision to restore to the Lord's Prayer the petition 'Lead us not into temptation' in its familiar form?

Familiarity may not breed contempt, but neither does it necessarily bring enlightenment. For many generations a stone horse-trough standing outside a hotel on the banks of the River Ouse at Bedford was a well-known local landmark. Passers-by came to regard it with comfortable affection, never understanding, until a clergyman visiting the hotel recognized it and restored it to its rightful place, that it was an ancient baptismal font.[1] How easily it had merged into the landscape! - how comfortably the time-honoured phrases of traditional liturgy pass us by!

2 *Worship with heart and mind*

Of course, there are times when the very familiarity of the words being said or sung releases the intellect and enables us to worship at the deeper level of the heart. Our faith cannot survive, however, without the counter-balance of a mind open to be nourished by the Lord's teaching. We heard in today's gospel his simple but profound response to the disciples' request to be taught to pray. Those few brief petitions conclude with the one which, in the oldest - and now in the latest - of the English versions, prays that we may not be led into temptation. How can we make rational sense of a phrase which, on the face of it, in no way corresponds to the nature of God as revealed in Jesus? It seems to suggest that, unless we ask him not to, God will lead us down a path that, at best, could severely shake our confidence in him and, at worst, might separate us from him altogether. Surely he never intends to entice us into sin; but neither does he cocoon us in cloistered isolation from a world in which temptation is inevitable. We need, therefore, to find a broader meaning for the word 'temptation'.

1. The font, which is probably of Saxon origin, can be seen in All Saints Church, Bedford.

3 *Strained to breaking point*

Let me take you, in imagination, to the old Chatham dockyard before the days of closure and redundancy. There, in the ropery, was a great machine on which six inch hempen hawsers made up of many strands were stretched to find their breaking point. By subjecting them to this test a safe working load was established for a rope's selection and use.

In biblical terms, to be tempted is not to be seduced but to be tested. The original petition, of which 'Lead us not into temptation' is hardly an accurate paraphrase, seeks not to avoid the testing but to be saved from breaking under it. We are asking God to stand by us in that particular trial and temptation which is ours, for temptation is usually a personal affair. It lies in wait and comes upon us, as it came upon our Lord, with sudden force, often striking at times of extreme vulnerability when we are physically and emotionally weak. There is no way of escaping from the ensuing struggle and tension; they are an essential part of the life of faith, and in facing up to them positively we shall become aware of their creative power.

4 *'Yes' to life*

Whatever the particular temptations that come our way, we have a working standard to follow in the example of Jesus. He has gone before us through the wilderness and the agony of Gethsemane, even to the supreme trial of the cross, always denying the possibility of escape or evasion, always affirming the possibility of victory. When we pray his prayer in sincerity and truth, we are saying 'Yes' to life itself.

PENTECOST 15

Direction of desire

John 3.30 (*AV*) *'He must increase and I must decrease.'*

1 *Distorted Obsessions*

A great deal of money must have been made in one way or another out of the seven deadly sins: anger, envy, avarice and, above all, pride are exploited to the full in television soap operas like *Dallas* and *Dynasty*, whilst much of the advertising during the commercial breaks is the very embodiment of lust, sloth and greed. Writers for the popular press and television are only too aware that stories of virtue rarely carry any news or entertainment value, whereas vice – especially in its more lurid forms – is an unfailing source of dramatic scripts and banner headlines.

The bizarre events portrayed in today's gospel would certainly qualify for a similar treatment by the media if they happened now. All the ingredients for a sensational write-up are present, and it is unlikely that the copy-writer would get far before he found himself using the word 'desire'. This story is full of it. A daughter's desire – at whatever shameful cost – to gratify a demanding mother. The mother's frenzied desire for vengeance against the one who had dared to threaten her position by a moral rebuke; the ruler's consuming desire not to lose face before his guests; each character's distorted obsession rooted in pride and branching out into anger and envy; all of them conspiring grotesquely to bring about the death of a courageous man.

When its destructive consequences are presented to us in such a dramatic way, we may come to regard desire as dangerous in itself, as many devout moralists have done before. They have seen it as something to be suppressed, even eradicated; but this is by no means the entire case.

2 *The heaven of reality*

The painter who deals only in realism – however starkly and graphically – can never convey the whole truth. There exists a higher level of perception at which an artist seeks to share his vision of what has been called the 'heaven of reality'. Opening our eyes to the rich potential of things seen against the background of eternity. It is a prophetic vision, having about it a fearless, self-giving quality that exalts the spirit and points us forward to a new and richer order of being.

The central character in the gospel narrative, although he is not seen alive, is the prophet John, in whom personal desire has been transmuted into a passionate longing for the coming of God's Kingdom. His call to the turbulent, sinful society of his time was not just 'Repent' but 'Repent, *for the Kingdom of Heaven is at hand*'. The man and his message stand in sharp contrast to the shameless self-indulgence of Herod's court. They point us from earth to heaven, revealing to us the ultimate truth about our desire.

3 *Pointing outwards*

'Desire is the emotional stimulus that sets in action all purposeful activity.' So writes Martin Israel in a passage about the Tenth Commandment.[2] And C. S. Lewis once made the suggestion that we do not desire enough. We are, he said '. . . like and ignorant child who wants to go on making mud pies in a slum because he cannot imagine what is meant by the offer of a holiday by the sea'.[3] Desire, it seems, is good and God-given but, as we learn from the characters in the drama of John's martyrdom, it can have tragic consequences. How are we to understand it?

1. From *Practical Mysticism for Normal People* by Evelyn Underhill.

2. From *Discipline of Love* by Martin Israel, Chapter 10, Page 89.

3. From a wartime sermon preached at Oxford by C.S. Lewis and quoted by Murdoch Dahl in his book *Sin Streamlined*, (Mowbrays, 1966).

Think of that most spectacular of modern inventions – the laser. It has transformed, to their great advantage, the work in a number of professions from surgery to surveying. Yet its use is always accompanied by severe warnings and restrictions. This is because a laser beam accidentally turned inwards upon the user destroys the cellular tissue and can cause blindness. Desire is likewise meant to go outward from the self: towards God in worship, towards our neighbour in loving service and towards all created things in reverence and delight. When it is turned inwards it creates the condition of self-centredness in which the deadly sins can flourish.

4 *Signposts*

The whole ministry of John the Baptist was like a signpost pointing away from himself towards the coming Saviour. He spoke of himself in relation to Jesus as the best man is to the bridegroom. 'He must increase and I must decrease', he said.

The scandal of the events leading up to his death provides a warning signpost pointing to the dangers of perverted desire. May we who see these signs in our own day be ever open to the power of God's grace to overcome our selfish desire and point us towards him, to whom be glory in the church and in Christ Jesus.

PENTECOST 16

Types of blindness

Luke 19.20 (*JB*) *'At his gate there lay a poor man called Lazarus.'*

1 *Seeing is believing*

Here are some words which, taken out of context, sound like a conundrum. 'Chips at twelve o'clock, peas at three o'clock and fish between nine and six'. In fact, they come from the moving account given by a blind girl, of the way in which she coped with the exigencies of day to day living.[1] Her helper at the meal table, by relating her plate to the face of a clock, enabled her not only to identify what she was about to eat, but also how to locate it. He was her interpreter, disclosing by this simple formula what was concealed from her, although everyone around could see it openly.

She was eventually to undergo a successful operation whereby she was able to see the world around her with her own eyes. Its impact was overwhelming. She recalls her sense of wonder at the incredible greenness of the grass which hitherto she had only felt through the soles of her shoes. She had to kneel down and touch it to make sure that it was what she had felt before. She saw it for the first time full of different shades of green. 'It's so marvellous, so beautiful', she exclaimed. At that level of vision the expression 'seeing is believing' strikes a new note; a note of depth and reality. We understand that something more than just physical sight is involved. 'I see', says the true artist, bringing to his picture that quality of inward meaning which conveys so much more than a photograph. 'I see', says the great physician with an intuitive sympathy that goes right to the root of the sickness. Just as there is more than one level of vision, so there are types of blindness that go beyond the

1. From *Emma and I*, by Sheila Hocken, (Gollancz).

physical, affecting the mind and the heart. In one of Chesterton's stories,[2] a murderer enters and leaves an apartment block openly in full view of the four men posted to watch its only entrance. Afterwards they were unanimous in their testimony that no one had gone in or out. What they meant was that no one *they could suspect* had done so. The murderer proved to be a postman, rendered mentally invisible by custom and familiarity. They saw him, but their seeing was so perfunctory and casual that it amounted to blindness.

2 *Culpable blindness*

In today's gospel parable, the beggar Lazarus sits at the gate of the mansion and is so much a part of the familiar background that he is rendered invisible to the mind and heart of Dives, the rich man within. Even in the life beyond death, when Dives is in torment, he continues to regard Lazarus as a menial; part of a familiar, natural and inevitable order of things. We are not told that he is especially evil nor that the beggar is especially virtuous. The story is not so much about culpable wickedness as about culpable blindness; it raises questions for us concerning the things that stand in the way of our growth and development as human beings in relation to God, to others, and to the world around us. With what eyes do we see them?

The eyes of Dives were blinded by a life of ease and security to the desperate plight of the beggar at his own gate. Christians are called to see through the eyes of Christ that when greed denies another's need there is an obligation to live more frugally and to give more freely.

The eyes of Dives were blinded by his wealth and status to the simple fact that Lazarus was a fellow human being. Christians are called to see through the eyes of Christ that in him, all differentials of class and worldly position are dis-

2. From the fifth tale in *The Innocence of Father Brown* entitled 'The Invisible Man'.

solved. No one is more or less important in Christ's eyes.

The eyes of Dives and his family were blinded to the means of grace provided by God. Christians are called day by day to receive new insights from the practice of their faith by word and sacrament. When they fail or grow slack their religion becomes a slavish, humdrum affair. 'If the doors of perception were cleansed', wrote William Blake, 'everything would appear to man as it is, infinite.'[3] His words find an echo in the poignant experience of the blind girl who received her sight and marvelled at the miracle of the green grass. Her story, too, is a kind of parable encouraging us to open our physical eyes to the freshness and wonder of God's creation, giving us a glimpse of the reality of heaven where . . .

We shall rest and we shall see,
We shall see and we shall love,
We shall love and we shall praise,
Behold what shall be in the end
and shall not end.[4]

PENTECOST 17

Simplicity of faith

Luke 7.8 (*AV*) '. . . *a man set under authority.*'

1 *An awesome question*

Young children have a unique knack of pinpointing truth in a way that brings us up short and tests our assumptions. They tend to do this artlessly, either by a simple question or by a disturbingly candid comment. Let us take one of each.

First a question from a little boy, the son of old-fashioned and devout parents, who invariably read him a bible story at

3. From 'The Marriage of Heaven and Hell'.
4. From *The City of God* by St. Augustine, Book XXII, Chapter 30.

bed-time. One night, after his mother had read to him from the gospels, his father came up to say a last goodnight. The boy fixed him with an unblinking gaze and asked, 'Daddy, did Jesus never talk about anything else except God?'

What an awesome question! If the image, not only in that boy's mind but in the mind of the innocents among any age-group, is of a Jesus who had no table-talk, no exchange of views on anything other than 'religion' (and by implication no *fun*!), then it is a false image; indeed it is a monstrous distortion of the truth. There are few things more likely to repel an honest enquirer than a so-called christian whose whole outlook is blinkered by his religious commitment; one who is deafened and deadened to all else but his particular way of believing. If our religion is based on a model of narrow-minded fanaticism, then that basis is not scriptural. The Christ of the gospels was not like that. Neither was he so immersed in a materialistic and secular approach to ministry that the godward dimension was swept away. He was committed to a vision of the Kingdom of God, and it is to the Kingdom that the gospel writers were pointing. Like the makers of a carefully designed tapestry, they selected and wove together the words and actions of Jesus to make a pattern that would find its place in the theology and liturgy of the early Church, as it does in ours. Pleasantry and small-talk - all the loose ends of casual conversation - are passed over. Hence the received impression behind the small boy's question.

2 *The pagan soldier*

Now to turn to another child - a little girl. Hers was not a question but an answer. She was asked the meaning of the word 'pagan', and her reply was clear and unhesitating; 'pagans are people who don't quarrel about religion'. Another telling comment, throwing into sinister relief all the wars that have been fought, and the conflicts that even now are raging, against a background of divided religious allegiance.

The girl's remark recalls us to the fact that this Sunday's gospel is about a pagan. It is not a passage in which Jesus talks directly about God; in fact it is the pagan who does most of the talking. He was a centurion – the equivalent of a senior warrant officer in a modern army; a man whose pattern of existence was governed, not by his formal homage to the various Roman gods, but by the demands of regular soldiering. On duty, off duty, on parade, on leave: there was an inevitable rhythm about a life committed to maintaining order and keeping the peace in an alien land. It is reminiscent of the regime experienced by the forces of the British Raj on the north-west frontier of India. Like one of them, he saw himself as a cog in a well-regulated military machine. Routine and efficiency were inescapable facts of life; his response to established authority was instinctive. In describing him as a pagan soldier, which is truly what he was, the emphasis mut be on the second word: it was as a soldier that he approached our Lord, on behalf of his sick servant, having a soldier's courage and integrity yet bound by the limits of an established order. 'Give the word', he said, 'and let my servant be cured. For I am under authority myself . . .'

3 *A prophetic vision*

If recent massive advances in science and technology have taught us anything, it must be that established orders can never be taken for granted. Never again can we look upon our universe as something settled and solid. The physicists have enabled us to see, as never before, our place in the ever-changing material order, and have revealed within it a potential undreamt of in past ages. Here are some words written by a great scientist, who was also a theologian and a priest, Teilhard de Chardin.

> We have discovered that a process without limit has brought into being the realms of substance and essence. Our fathers supposed themselves to go back no further

than yesterday, each man containing within himself the ultimate value of his existence. They held themselves to be confined within the limits of their years and their corporeal frame. We have blown asunder this narrow compass and those beliefs.[1]

In these terms, the reaction of the centurion to Jesus was in its way prophetic. He had made a discovery which took him beyond the conventional view of his existence and gave it a wider meaning. In a primitive way he was foreshadowing Teilhard's great vision of Jesus as the crown of evolution, the Christ of the universe. It was his perception of authority that led him to the deeper truth, and he responded with a directness and simplicity which is occasionally reflected in the comments of the very young.

The practice of religion can so easily become overlaid with complications and conflict that we need constantly to be recalled to the straightforwardness and simplicity of true faith. It is to the credit of those who compiled our liturgy that, in *The Alternative Service Book*, they have adapted for us to use, in that precious moment before the distribution of the bread and the wine, the words of a pagan soldier who encountered Christ: 'Lord, I am not worthy to receive you, but only say the word, and I shall be healed.'[2]

PENTECOST 18

Use it or lose it

Matthew 6.19 (*NEB*) *'Do not store up for yourselves treasure on earth.'*

'Going . . . going . . .' – the discreet voice of the auctioneer murmurs across the sale-room; 'Going at one hundred and

1. P. Teilhard de Chardin, *The Future of Man*, (Fontana, 1969), p.17.
2. *The Alternative Service Book*, (Oxford/Mowbray, 1980), p.172.

fifty thousand pounds, one hundred and fifty thousand. All done?' There is a pause before the hammer descends, and a violin by Stradivarius has changed hands. Because of the immense cost of insuring it under any terms, it will now be taken from the auction to a secure repository, there to be locked away and rarely played in public. It is a sad reflection upon a society obsessed with wealth and ownership that such a sequence of events can take place. Violins were made for their music to be heard. What a tragedy when, in the cause of safe-keeping, they are entombed!

A secure repository in biblical times could simply be a hole in the ground. More than one archaeologist has uncovered a cache of ancient valuables, carefully wrapped and interred for safe-keeping. In today's gospel parable three men are entrusted with responsibility for part of their master's wealth. The first two were not afraid to venture it profitably in trade; whilst the third, acting on the dubious principle that if you do not enter the race you cannot lose, buried his single share in the ground. He shrank from the implications of his stewardship, and it is from his attitude and from his ultimate condemnation that we may draw a threefold message – under the headings possession, power, and paradox.

1 *Possession*

Some words are like weather-vanes: according to prevailing conditions they may point to opposite poles of meaning. The ancient and biblical word 'mammon', standing for wealth and property, is such a word. Sometimes it is used in the sense of *that which is entrusted*, just as the master in the parable entrusted a proportion of talents to each servant (we entrust our prayers to God with a contraction of the same word – 'Amen'); sometimes it takes on the ominous meaning of *that which is trusted in*. In short, mammon is either a slave or a master. Money and material goods are necessary facts of life: it is the way we possess them that dictates their meaning. The third servant chose the negative way of supposing that something can be truly possessed by hoarding it. He was sadly mistaken. The condition of abundant life prevails when our attitude to mammon has shifted from attachment to detachment.

2 *Power*

'When the I, the Me and the Mine are dead, the work of the Lord is done,' wrote one of the great holy men of India.[1] The turning of man's energies inwards towards the demands and appetites of the self alone is of the very nature of sin. So it is the typical stance of sin – half cowering and half defiant – that we see in the third servant standing before his master as he gives an account of his stewardship. He assumed that the master was a tyrant. How wrong he was! How wrong we are if we approach our calling as christians fearfully, as a task imposed by a demanding God – something extraneous to the main business of our lives. It is from within that God calls us and entrusts us with his resources. They are *his* resources, and we handle them in the power of *his* spirit. Whether or not his loving purpose will be realized depends upon our willingness to be open to his power working in and through us. We have no need to be fearful. He has said, 'My grace is sufficient for you'.

3 *Paradox*

The 'punch line' of the parable contains a terrible paradox: 'To everyone who has will be given more . . . but from the man who has not, even what he has will be taken away.' It was the servant given least who was condemned. By failing to make use even of the resources he had, he forfeited everything.

The warning is clear. It was echoed in the post office

1. From *One Hundred Poems of Kabir*, Trans. Rabindranath Tagore & Evelyn Underhill, 1915.

slogan of the early 1980s, when sub post offices were in danger of closing through lack of custom; 'Use it or lose it!' If christians treat their faith as a private acquisition to be taken home and locked away, there will be for the Church, as there was for the cowardly servant, and awful day of reckoning. Like a limb which has atrophied through lack of exercise, we shall find that our power has gone and we have nothing to give to a world in desperate need.

The wealth of the christian gospel has been given to us to be given away. It is 'good news for men in all the earth'[2] to be poured forth in love like the music of a great instrument played by an artist devoted to the music. When that happens, a shining paradox appears, for we discover that the riches of Christ, when they are shared, do not diminish like the treasures of the sale-room, but rather increase to his glory.

2. E.J. Burns, from the hymn 'Good News', No. 98 in *A Hundred Hymns for Today*, (Hymns Ancient & Modern Ltd., 1969).

PENTECOST 19

Finding a vantage point

> Luke 19.4 (*NEB*) '. . . *he climbed a sycamore tree in order to see* . . . '

1 *A strange and humbling experience*

It was during the hot, dry summer of 1976 that the churchwarden of a country parish in Essex climbed to the top of the church tower and looked out upon something he had never been able to see before. The church had been build in Victorian times on part of the fourteenth century monastic site,[1] now completely hidden below the surface of

1. A college of Augustinian canons at Pleshey in Essex, founded in 1394 by Thomas, Duke of Gloucester, Uncle to Richard II.

the churchyard and its adjoining glebe. The warden had a strong sense of history: many times, mowing the churchyard grass, he had remarked to himself that there beneath his feet – if only he could see them – were the ancient foundations. His moment of revelation came with the drought of that year. The long weeks without rain had so parched the turf and shrunk the sub-soil that, as he looked down from his vantage point on the tower, he could see the whole outline of the old structure laid out before him. It was a strange and humbling experience to view himself and his own church superimposed upon an older and much larger ground-plan. It gave him an impression of being located in a stream of history. How modest was his own place in it, and yet how significant! Then he realized that if he had remained at ground level he could never have come to this moment of revelation, for down there the pattern from the past was still invisible. He had needed a different perspective from which to perceive new truth.

2 *The satellite view*

Consider the vantage points which have become accessible to man since the days when he built towers and battlements to the glory of God and in the cause of his own security. Scientific discovery, motivated by commercialism and curiosity – and with more than half an eye on the defence possibilities – has taken him further and further from ground level. Today, by means of rocket and satellite, he is given a perspective of the earth as a whole. He is awakened to the truth that his world can be viewed quite literally and physically as a global village. He is allowed to see his creatureliness in a way that, if he will respond, can challenge him and soften his heart towards his needy neighbours. There, laid out before him, is that to which he belongs, *not* that which belongs to him.

3 *The tree-top a place of revelation*

Sometimes it is by being lifted to another level physically that a graphic and life-changing inner vision can come. The dramatic vista to be seen from a space vehicle or even from the basket of a hot air balloon will be denied to most of us but, as we hear in today's gospel, a simple tree-top will serve to open a man's eyes to new truth.

The sycamore tree of Palestine, unlike the species of maple known in Britain by the same name, is a fig-mulberry with thick foliage. Its lower branches are only a short distance from the ground, making it easy to climb. An ideal point of vantage for a small man prompted by curiosity to see over the heads of a crowd. The particular sycamore from which Zaccheus looked down upon the face of Christ must have become for him like Jacob's stone pillow at Bethel, a lasting monument to a moment of revelation. In that place it was revealed to him what he was capable of becoming.

4 *A place of epiphany*

If he had stayed at ground level – this lonely man, whose way of life was motivated by commercialism and the acquisition of wealth – Christ would have remained both physically and spiritually invisible to him. By making a deliberate effort to gain the vantage point of the sycamore (and incidentally putting at risk more than just his physical security) he encountered the Lord and heard his call. That first foothold on the lowest branch proved to be an initial step on the way to self-knowledge, to contrition and thence to an attitude of outgoing generosity towards his neighbours.

Is it fanciful to suppose that in later years Zaccheus returned from time to time to his sycamore tree as to a place of vision and renewal? Each of us needs what one writer has called 'a place of God's epiphany';[2] a vantage point away

2. From *The World is a Wedding* by A.M. Allchin, (Darton, Longman & Todd), p.20.

from the unrelenting round of affairs carried on at 'ground level', where the things that motivate our lives can be re-appraised and measured against eternal values. Let us make a deliberate effort to find our own 'sycamore tree', where like Zaccheus we can become aware of the contrast between what we call living and life itself.

PENTECOST 20

True and false fruit

> Matthew 7.16 (*NEB*) '*you will recognise them by the fruits they bear.*'

1 *The promise of the seed*

What a formidable assortment of factual information has come our way in the last three decades, with the upsurge of popular interest in quiz games and quiz books! Here is a paperback containing no less than eight hundred and fify-five questions designed to test the reader's knowledge of bible facts, many of them concentrating on some aspect of its natural history![1] One section draws upon the wealth of references throughout scripture to different varieties of tree: pomegranate, almond, olive and apple all figure in the answers, recalling the promise of creation in Genesis that the earth should produce trees bearing fruit with their seed inside (Genesis 1.11). How richly that promise was fulfilled so that the cycle of natural growth from planting to harvesting came to be invested by the ancient writers with mystical significance. The child who carefully plants the pip from his harvest apple and allows his imagination to leap forward across the stages of growth – his own and the tree's – to the time when he will pick the fruit, is sharing in a primal vision

1. *The Bible Quiz Book*, (Collins, 1961).

of human existence. A behavioural scientist who is also a theologian, Sam Keen, takes up the same theme when he writes 'In the first green of life there is an announcement of intention. Birth contains a hidden promise of fulfilment; in the beginning is the end. The acorn promises the oak: the child, the man; potentiality looks forward to actuality. All life in its inception bears within it the promise of perfection.'[2] When Jesus issued his warning against the pedlars of false religious teaching he used the same analogy; 'you will recognise them', he said, 'by the fruits they bear'. The end product of a cycle that begins with the planting of a seed and matures through its various stages from greenness to ripeness will give you a clue to the plant's true identity. Growth, development and change are all part of the process.

2 *'Fruits' hung on the branches*

The Norway spruce produces its fruit only at rare intervals. On the large, forest-size trees, when the tight green chain-mail of the seed pods appears it makes a handsome embellishment to the branches, but if cones should ripen on a smaller specimen, they are likely to be stripped away to preserve its symmetry and therefore its market value as a Christmas tree. The bells and baubles and bright lights which then adorn the branches are hung on from without; they have their rightful place in the seasonal festivities but they are no part of the natural process of growth from within. Beautiful and fitting in their place but not the true fruit.

3. *Finding our true identity*

One of the great nineteenth century children's classics *The Adventures of Pinocchio*, is the story of an animated puppet, bearing within himself the capacity to become fully human. On the eve of Pinocchio's achieving his heart's desire to be

2. *To a Dancing God* by Sam Keen, (Fontana, 1971), p.89.

changed into a real boy, there is a poignant sequence in which he is forced to spend a whole night out in the open, storm-tossed and shivering, a victim of his own folly. Just when he is fainting with hunger, a tray is brought containing a loaf of bread, a roast chicken and four ripe apricots.

> The puppet was much comforted at the sight of the good things but when he began to eat them what was his disgust at finding the bread was plaster, the chicken cardboard and the four apricots painted alabaster![3]

Poor Pinocchio! His frustration at having to wait so long for food which, when it came, was counterfeit and gave him no nourishment, reflects our own predicament when we put our whole trust in man-made techniques and systems and ignore the authentic source of life, the action of the Spirit in our hearts. Remember St Paul's fervent prayer to the Father 'that he may grant you strength and power through his Spirit *in your inner being*, that through faith Christ may dwell *in your hearts* in love (Ephesians 3.16). Each of us bears within us the capacity to become fully human, to grow and develop in response to that divine love radiating outwards from the heart. And yet, so often we choose to seek our identity in external things, in the status and possessions that are 'hung on' from without. They leave us feeling restless and estranged; in exile from our true centre. Like Adam banished from the loving harmony of Eden.

The Bible begins with the tree of Adam's downfall in Genesis (3.12) and ends with the tree of life yielding one crop of fruit each month of which, says the writer of Revelation, the leaves serve for the healing of the nations (23.2). In between is the story of God's inestimable love in the redemption of the world by our Lord Jesus Christ. It summons us away from a shallow identity which glosses over or ignores the seed of divine love received into the depths of our being. A seed that carries within it the

3. *The Adventures of Pinocchio* by Carlo Collodi, Chapter 29, (published in translation by J.M. Dent & Sons).

character of the whole plant and will, if we are open to the development and change involved, mature towards the measure of the stature of the fullness of Christ.

PENTECOST 21

Finding unity in Christ's presence

John 11.21 (*NEB*) '*Martha said to Jesus "If you had been here Sir, my brother would not have died".* '

1 *Two words are enough*

One of the most momentous verses in scripture is also the shortest. It occurs in the eleventh chapter of St John in the passage immediately following upon the gospel for today. The thirty-fifth verse consists of two words only, 'Jesus wept'. Like many another grief-stricken mourner standing by the graveside of one who has been dearly loved, Jesus wept at the tomb of his friend Lazarus. What else can a man do when he is moved to the very depths by the agony of bereavement? Words are so inadequate to express the deepest feelings.

How misguided of those television interviewers, microphone in hand at the scene of a disaster, inviting someone facing the shock of sudden bereavement to describe their feelings! The tumult of conflicting emotions in the face of tragedy cannot possibly be articulated verbally. The whole truth of any situation, tragic or not, can never be put into words, only some small part of it. Deep sorrow or love or faith, the 'timeless moment' of profound inward vision; these things, because they sound the very depths of our being, lead us away from words. It is therefore fitting that this significant verse of scripture should be brief; 'Jesus wept'. Two words are enough; the rest cannot be conveyed.

2 *The experience of mourning*

Yet those two words taken in their context spell out a message for us in a world that is becoming day by day more divided and torn by conflict. A world which is destroying its own wholeness and harmony because it cannot see that the answer to its problems does not lie either in a spate of words or a torrent of retaliatory action. Somehow, we who are called to show forth the kingdom that Christ came to proclaim, must begin to enter into his experience of mourning at the grave of Lazarus.

'To know mourning and pity', writes Rowan Williams, 'makes domineering and self-assertion unthinkable. Sensitivity to the depth and presence of others in their vulnerability rules out the bitter and harsh struggle for power in which others are made to pay the price of our fears and insecurities.'[1]

Our Lord was able to weep and bear silently the pain not only of bereavement but of all the abuse and aggression that brought him to the cross. We are called to stand with him partaking more and more in the suffering around us and offering it to God inwardly and inarticulately, never passing it back in retaliation.

3 *Hope in the darkness*

We have considered that momentous verse of two words which follows on from today's gospel, let us now turn to a significant word of only two letters occurring within the passage itself. It is the word 'if'. 'If you had been here Sir', said Martha to Jesus, 'my brother would not have died.' It sounds at first like a rebuke to him for arriving late, disturbingly reminiscent of all those personal 'ifs' with which we reproach ourselves. If such and such had been done or said concerning our health, our work, our relationship or whatever, things might be different, we tell our-

1. *The Truce of God*, Rowan Williams, (Fount, 1983), chapter 51, pp.86-7.

selves, attributing our anxiety or unhappiness to that 'if'. The path of disappointment then becomes a cul-de-sac, because we cannot see beyond the dead end of 'if'. It was not so with Martha. Hers was not the negative language of reproach – 'If *only* you had come in time' – but the positive language of faith and confidence that in the presence of Christ, though we walk through the valley of the shadow, we can face the future with hope; 'If you had been here Sir, my brother would not have died. *Even now I know* that whatever you ask of God, God will grant you'. Can we not, in imagination, enter into her encounter with the Lord, sharing in that moment of crisis and drawing out her words to meet our own darkness of disappointment. 'If you had been here, Lord, your healing presence, your special relationship with God and with us would have made the difference between life and death. You Lord were the missing dimension, the only one who could have made sense of it all, and without you we can find neither hope nor meaning.'

4 *Getting it together*

There is a phrase in the modern vernacular standing for the achievement of order and unity which speaks of 'getting it together' or 'getting one's act together'. How expressive it is of the need to reconcile the tragic divisions we see in the world around us and in our own lives. The various elements in society seem to be running on parallel lines with unbridgeable gaps between. How are we to reconcile the plight of certain victims of starvation with the civil war that rages around them and prevents their being fed? Or the fervent allegiance of groups loyal to a particular religion with the inhuman atrocities committed in its name? It is a basic tenet of artistic perspective that a third dimension can be represented in the drawing of parallel lines by leading them towards a point of convergence. There has to be a centre, a point of unity for our world and for us as individuals. Our parallel lines of occupation, family, leisure and so on must converge to disclose a single meaning.

Without the dimension given in us and through us by the presence of Christ, we cannot 'get our act together'. Yet we try to cure our sense of failure by filling up our lives with a continuous succession of projects and pleasures until a tragedy pulls us up short and we find ourselves standing as Jesus did at a graveside and there is nothing to say or do but weep. It may be, in receiving that gift of tears, we are brought into closer unity with him who is the resurrection and the life of all creation.

PENTECOST 22

Decisive Discipleship

Philippians 3.14 (*AV*) '*I press towards the mark for the prize of the high calling of God in Christ Jesus.*'

1 *No visible landmark*

This book has been written in a part of East Anglia where the landscape has suffered drastic change by the removal of hedges and ditches to make way for large-scale arable farming. Fields merge into wide plains sometimes stretching as far as the eye can see. One can imagine the ghost of an old Suffolk ploughman returning from a previous century to stand aghast at the disappearance of familiar landmarks and wondering with dismay how his horse-drawn plough could ever cut a straight furrow without some visible point at which to aim his team. The old ploughman and the modern golfer driving off from the tree have something in common; both must line up on a distant mark while at the same time keeping an eye on what is immediately in front of their feet. They are lost without the constant point of reference given in one case by a distant tree, in the other by the flag at the green.

2 *A resourceful scoundrel*

Their vital need for a sense of direction symbolizes the predicament of a man who finds that, because of a drastic change in his circumstances, the familiar landmarks in his life are in danger of disappearing. The dishonest steward in today's gospel was such a man. Without a clear and resolute aim, he would have ended up outcast and desolate; that is why he took the prompt and resourceful action for which he was commended. The fact that what he did was totally self-centred and amounted to an unscrupulous confidence trick, is not the point of the story. A local incident still fresh in the minds of his hearers may well have given Jesus a talking point to which the parable could be related most effectively. The central character was a resourceful scoundrel who acted decisively and promptly to secure his own ends; Christ needs resourceful saints who for his sake, when the crisis comes, will display those same qualities of decision and promptness.

3 *The need for landscaping*

A journey from the wide horizons of East Anglia to some overcrowded inner city precinct can provide a study in contrasts and yet reveal a common deprivation. Both are in need of landscaping. The skyline laid bare by massive industrial farming cries out to be broken up by some natural feature to relieve the eye. The cramped cheek-by-jowl urban housing sorely needs an enlargement of outlook by being placed in a wider context. We are reminded that the old ploughman intent upon his furrow, and the golfer assiduously keeping his eye on the ball, must both be able to lift their heads towards the distant mark. In the same way, the mind and spirit of Christ's followers have to be landscaped and their actions given a clear direction if they are not to be at a loss in the moment of crisis. The zeal and energy of the rascally steward, like that of any man who applies himself resolutely to a clear goal, whether at work or at leisure, is an example to be followed in the realm of faithful discipleship. We have our reference point in Christ incarnate, crucified and risen, and now present with us through his Spirit; let us be alert for his coming to us afresh every day of our lives. 'Direct, control, suggest this day, all I design or do or say; all my powers with all their might, in thy sole glory may unite.'[1]

4 *Stirring up the will*

The collect for this Sunday asks God to stir up our wills to do his will. In the original Latin[2] it begins with the word *Excita*, suggesting urgency and immediacy and reminding us of the brisk enterprise of the steward in the parable. It sounds an alarm bell in the ranks of those christians who have accepted a lethargic *status quo* and are hesitant about taking prompt and positive action on the issues that threaten today's world and therefore challenge today's Church.

LAST SUNDAY AFTER PENTECOST

Hope and fulfilment

> Psalm 130 (*AV*) '*I wait for the Lord, my soul doth wait, and in his word do I hope.*'

Today we have arrived at a watershed in the christian calendar. This is the last of the long season of Sundays after Pentecost; a moment for reflection and re-appraisal. Next Sunday, according to the ASB lectionary, will be the ninth before Christmas; a time for the awakening of fresh hope as we look forward to celebrating the fulfilment of God's promise in the birth of Christ.

1. From a morning hymn by Bishop Thomas Ken (1637–1711) beginning 'Awake my Soul'.

2. St Gregory's version (590).

1 *Anticipating the feast*

On secular calendars, however, the forthcoming weeks will be ordered differently. Before long, if it has not already begun, there will be widespread anticipation of the festive season in shops, offices, schools and hospitals. An air of excitement and celebration will prevail well before Christmas itself, with mutual good wishes and hopes for 'All the best' being expressed on all sides.

2 *Symbols of joy and hope*

This pre-Christmas *bonhomie* is very like the atmosphere surrounding most weddings. The customary routines and restraints of every day are laid aside in a spirit of celebration. We share in the joy of the bride and groom at the promise of fulfilment in their new life together. Perhaps we especially enjoy a wedding because, like the revelry at Christmas, it speaks to some deep need within us for festivity and ritual. Perhaps we especially enjoy Christmas because, like the vows that are made and the toasts that are drunk at a wedding, it stirs in our restless hearts some positive hope of renewal and fulfilment. The wedding invitation, like the Christmas card, can be for us a symbol of joy and hope.

3 *'If you can wait and not be tired by waiting'*[2]

A somewhat dubious piece of popular folklore suggests that it is the bride's prerogative to be a little late for the wedding. We heard in the gospel how the modern roles were reversed in first-century Palestine. It was the bridegroom who reserved the right to keep guests and bridal party waiting until he arrived at an unspecified hour (and with a minimum of advance warning) to 'capture' his bride and carry her off to their new home. Then followed the ceremony, signalling

1. For the development of this theme, see *The Feast of Fools* by Harvey Cox, Introduction, pp.7ff.

2. Rudyard Kipling, from the ballad 'If'.

a time of joyous celebration. The privilege of attending the feast belonged to those who, because of their vigilance in waiting and their preparedness to accompany him, were on the spot when the bridegroom arrived. This homely, happy sequence of events provided the groundwork for our Lord's parable. The joy of the wedding breakfast is a sign of the Kingdom of God; the time of waiting in vigilance and expectancy for the coming of the bridegroom, reveals the quality of christian hope.

4 *The best is yet to come*

When pre-Christmas partygoers raise their glasses to wish each other 'All the Best', they are usually expressing a hope for prosperity or success in wordly terms. Conversely, the expression 'Hope for the best' often bears witness to an underlying fear of failure or disappointment. Neither expression comprehends the true nature of the christian's hope in the promises of God. It is no mere optimism, but a deep and joyful confidence which is linked in scripture with faith and love and is prepared, not for the worst, but for the best in terms of our eternal destiny.

On this particular Sunday the parable of the bridesmaids is reminding us that we stand at a juncture, waiting like them for the beginning of the feast. The contrast between the monotony of their long, drawn-out vigil and the sudden excitement of the bridegroom's arrival, can sharpen our sense of longing for the approach of the Lord and enable us to prepare for it with hope; not a superficial hope which falsely acclaims his coming before the time, but the hope – not self-induced but received from him – that all our future, for better or worse, is in his hands.